Nuwave Oven Recipes

Anyone Can Learn

By: TAK Publishing

NUWAVE OVEN RECIPES ANYONE CAN LEARN

TAK Publishing
179 South Main Street
Gardner, MA 01440 U.S.A

ISBN – 978-0-9826947-8-7

Note: This book contains the opinions and ideas of its author. It is intended to provide helpful and informative material on the subject matter covered. It is sold with the understanding that the author and publisher are not engaged in rendering professional services in the book. If the reader requires personal assistance or advice, a competent professional should be consulted.

The author and publisher specifically disclaim any responsibility for any liability, loss, or risk, personal or otherwise, which is incurred as a consequence, directly or indirectly, of the use and application of any of the contents of this book.

We are not affiliated with the makers of the Nuwave Oven or Hearthware, Inc. These are our own recipes.

Welcome to Nuwave Oven Recipes Anyone Can Learn!

Here you will find over 250 Recipes for your Nuwave Oven. Just as a note some of the recipes in this book contain recipes for all different meals and the instructions sometimes say cook them to our desired doneness. Cooking times and Power Levels may need to be adjusted according to your desired doneness.

I have tried a lot of these recipes and they were delicious. So thumb through, find a recipe that interests you and give it a whirl. Please note that all Nuwave Ovens are different and the power level may need to need to be adjusted. I did most recipes on the highest power setting since a lot these recipes were converted from recipes I do in my own oven and Hi is the closest equivalent to the temperature.

Here are a few Nuwave Tips

- I would suggest starting your Nuwave Oven on a lower setting and raising it if it is not cooking fast enough.

- Now that the Nuwave Oven has a Baking Kit many of the recipes can now be cooked in these making Nuwave cooking a lot easier.

- Many of these recipes require stovetop cooking while your main dish is cooking in your Nuwave.

- I have included dessert recipes and have found that cookie recipes along with some meat recipes need to done in multiple batches. Cookies take a bit longer to do than in the oven but I have found I like not to have to heat up my oven.

- Most Nuwave Ovens come with a very handy cooking guide, if you think that my time on a recipe may be off I would suggest referring to the guide.

- If you are cooking things that you want crispy remove it from the Nuwave Oven immediately or steam could build up and make your food soggy.

- The key to great Nuwave cooking is timing. I would suggest you play with these recipes and male them your own. Everyone's tastes are different so you might like something cooked a bit more or less than I do.

- Some of these recipes contain meats or items that could drip. To save myself some clean up I place tin foil under the food to catch any drippings.

- I may not be as well versed in Nuwave cooking as most people and I rarely ever play around with the rack heights so if it may be worth it to try some of these recipes at different heights. Usually the lowest rack setting will do.

Table of Contents

Beef

Breakfast

Dessert

Pork

Poultry

Seafood

Vegetables

Holiday Favorites

Beef

Asian Steaks
Makes 4 servings

Ingredients
4 steaks
1/8 cup lime juice
1/4 cup orange juice
1/2 cup fresh mint, chopped
1/4 cup low sodium soy sauce
2 tablespoons fresh ginger, minced
2 tablespoons jalapeno, minced
3 cloves of garlic

Directions
1. Combine steak and all ingredients in a large heavy-duty zip top bag. Refrigerate sealed bag for 8-12 hours, turning once. Freezes well at this point also.
2. Remove steak from bag, reserving marinade. Place on 4 inch rack and cook for 6-7 minutes per side for medium-rare.
3. Refer to cooking guide for all other temperatures. Baste the steak with marinade when you turn the meat. Let meat rest 4-5 minutes before cutting.

Baked Beef Stew
Makes 8 servings
Cook Time: 2 Hrs

Ingredients
2 pounds beef stew meat, cut into 1 inch cubes
1 (14.5 ounce) can diced tomatoes with juice
1 cup water
3 tablespoons instant tapioca
1 tablespoon beef bouillon granules
2 teaspoons white sugar
1 1/2 teaspoons salt
1/4 teaspoon ground black pepper
4 carrots, cut into 1 inch pieces
2 strips celery, cut into 3/4 inch pieces
3 potato, peeled and cubed
1 onion, roughly chopped
1 slice bread, cubed

Directions
1. Lightly grease a 9x13 inch baking dish.
2. In a large skillet over medium heat, brown the stew meat; drain and set aside.
3. In a mixing bowl, combine the tomatoes, water, tapioca, beef bouillon granules, sugar, salt and pepper. Stir in the beef, carrots, celery, potatoes, onion, and bread cubes. Pour into the prepared baking dish.
4. Cover and bake on Hi for 2 hours, or until meat and vegetables are tender.

Barbecued Beef Ribs for Two
Makes 2 servings
Cook Time: 50 Min

Ingredients
2 pounds beef back ribs
1/2 cup ketchup
2 tablespoons finely chopped onion
2 garlic cloves, minced
2 tablespoons vinegar
1 tablespoon brown sugar
1/2 teaspoon chili powder
1/2 teaspoon Worcestershire sauce
1/8 teaspoon garlic powder
1 dash hot pepper sauce

Directions
1. Cut ribs into serving-size pieces; place in a large kettle and cover with water. Simmer, uncovered, for 50-60 minutes or until tender.
2. Meanwhile, combine remaining ingredients in a small saucepan. Simmer, uncovered, for 10 minutes.
3. Drain ribs; place in a greased shallow baking dish. Cover with sauce. Bake on Hi for 50-60 minutes.

Beef Brisket with Pearl Onions
Makes 8 servings

Ingredients
4 pounds beef brisket
1 (1 ounce) envelope dry onion soup mix
1 (10.25 ounce) jar Smucker's® Concord Grape Low Sugar Jelly
1 (12 ounce) jar Crosse & Blackwell® Seafood Cocktail Sauce
2 tablespoons butter
1 (6 ounce) package fresh sliced portobello mushrooms
1 (16 ounce) package frozen, white pearl onions, defrosted
2 tablespoons fresh tarragon, chopped

Directions
1. Place sheet of heavy-duty aluminum foil in a shallow roasting pan with foil extending 6 inches beyond pan on either side. Spray with no-stick cooking spray. Place the brisket fat-side down in middle of the foil.
2. Combine dry onion soup mix with jelly and cocktail sauce in a medium bowl. Pour half of mixture over the brisket; turn brisket fat-side up covering with remaining onion mixture. Bring both sides of foil to the middle and fold foil down on itself several times. Repeat with the two remaining sides. Bake on Hi for 3 hours or until fork-tender.
3. In a 10 inch skillet over medium heat, melt 2 tablespoons of butter; saute onions and mushrooms for 5-8 minutes or until light golden brown.
4. Remove brisket from pan; pour off juices skimming the fat off the top. Remove layer of fat from brisket. Slice meat across the grain into 1/4 inch thick slices. Return meat to roaster. Top the meat with the mushroom mixture, meat juices, and tarragon. Cover with foil. If needed reheat in your oven to before serving.

Beef Chimichangas
Makes 6 servings
Cook Time: 25 Min

Ingredients
1 pound ground beef
1 small onion, chopped
1 clove garlic, minced
1/2 teaspoon taco seasoning mix, or more to taste
1 teaspoon dried oregano
1/4 cup sour cream
1 (4 ounce) can chopped green chilies
2 tablespoons distilled white vinegar
1 cup shredded Cheddar cheese
1/4 cup margarine
6 (7 inch) corn tortillas

Directions
1. Brown the ground beef, onion, garlic, taco seasoning, and oregano in a skillet over medium heat, breaking the meat up into crumbles as it cooks, about 8 minutes.
2. Drain off excess fat. Stir in sour cream, chilies, and vinegar until well mixed. Remove from heat, and mix in the Cheddar cheese. Melt margarine in a small skillet over low heat. When melted, dip each tortilla into the margarine for about 30 seconds, or until soft.
3. Place the softened tortilla onto a baking sheet, and fill with about 1/3 cup of the meat mixture. Fold the right and left sides of the tortilla over the filling, then the top and bottom, making an envelope that completely encloses the filling. Flip the tortilla seam side down on the baking sheet. Repeat with remaining tortillas and filling.
4. Bake on Hi until the tortilla is crisp, about 15 minutes.

Beef Jerky
Makes 6 servings

Ingredients
1 pound of beef (any kind) I use brisket and cut while frozen
2 tablespoons brown sugar
1/3 cup of Worcestershire Sauce
1/2 cup soy sauce
1-1/4 teaspoon of garlic powder
1-1/4 teaspoons of onion powder
2-1/4 teaspoons of ground pepper
1 teaspoon liquid smoke (optional)

Directions
1. Place all the above ingredients into a large freezer bag or large bowl. Let marinate for 4-8 hours in refrigerator.
2. Place pieces of meat on liner pan and 4 inch rack (when using 2inch rack you can use 3 different levels). Do not let meat touch. Dehydrate on 3 for about 3 hours.
3. Half way through the process I move the beef to different racks.
4. Tent the dome during the last 5 minutes.
5. Pat excess moisture with paper towel, cool, and store.

Beef Kabobs
Makes 4 servings

Ingredients
1/2 cup soy sauce
1/4 cup water
3 tablespoons thinly sliced green onions
2 tablespoons lemon juice
2 tablespoons honey
2 teaspoons minced garlic
1 (1 1/2 pound) lean boneless beef top round or sirloin steak, cut into 1/2 inch to 1 inch thick cubes (about 16 pieces)
Fresh or canned pineapple chunks (about 16)
1 large green pepper (seeded and each cut in eight 1-inch inch chunks)
8 small mushrooms
2 onions cut into chunks
4 metal skewers or wooden (soak wooden in water for 1 hour to avoid burning)

Directions
1. Mix all marinade ingredients in a large bowl. Add beef; cover and marinate in refrigerator at least 8 hours, stirring several times.
2. Drain beef; reserve marinade for basting.
3. Alternately thread pineapple, beef and vegetables on each skewer.
4. Place kabobs on 4 inch cooking rack. Cook on power level HI for 4-6 minutes, turn, baste with reserved marinade and cook an additional 4-6 minutes on power level HI depending on desired doneness.

Beef Potpie
Makes 2 servings
Cook Time: 25 Min

Ingredients
1 tablespoon butter or margarine
1 teaspoon dried minced onion
1 tablespoon all-purpose flour
1/8 teaspoon pepper
2/3 cup beef stock
1 cup frozen mixed vegetables, thawed
1/2 cup cubed cooked roast beef
1 egg
2 tablespoons milk
1/2 cup biscuit/baking mix

Directions
1. In a small saucepan, melt butter. Add onion and cook for 1 minute. stir in flour and pepper until blended. Gradually whisk in broth. Bring to a boil; cook and stir for 2 minutes or until thickened. Stir in vegetables and beef; heat through. Transfer to two greased 10-oz. custard cusp.
2. In a bowl, combine egg and milk. Stir in biscuit mix until smooth. Spoon evenly over meat mixture. Place on an ungreased baking sheet.
3. Cook on Hi for 25-30 minutes or until bubbly and top is golden brown.

Beef Sirloin Tip Roast
Makes 10 servings
Cook Time: 2 Hrs 30 Min

Ingredients
1 (3 pound) sirloin tip roast
1 1/4 cups water, divided
1 (8 ounce) can mushroom stems and pieces, drained
1 envelope onion soup mix
3 tablespoons cornstarch

Directions
1. Place a large piece of heavy-duty foil (21-in. x 17-in.) in a shallow roasting pan. Place roast on foil. Pour 1 cup water and mushrooms over roast. Sprinkle with soup mix.
2. Wrap foil around roast; seal tightly. Cook on Hi 2-1/2 to 3 hours or until meat reaches desired doneness (for medium-rare, a meat thermometer should read 145 degrees F; medium, 160 degrees F; well-done, 170 degrees F).
3. Remove roast to a serving platter and keep warm. Pour drippings and mushrooms into a saucepan.
4. Combine cornstarch and remaining water until smooth; gradually stir into drippings. Bring to a boil; cook and stir for 2 minutes or until thickened. Serve with slice beef.

Beef Tenderloin with Potatoes
Makes 10 servings
Cook Time: 1 Hr

Ingredients
2 1/4 cups water
1 1/2 cups ketchup
3 (.7 ounce) packages Italian salad dressing mix
1 tablespoon prepared mustard
3/4 teaspoon Worcestershire sauce
1 (3 pound) whole beef tenderloin
10 medium potatoes, peeled and quartered
1/2 cup butter or margarine, melted
1/2 teaspoon salt
1/4 teaspoon pepper

Directions
1. Combine the first five ingredients in a large resealable plastic bag. Pierce tenderloin in several places; place in bag and turn to coat. Seal and refrigerate for 8 hours or overnight.
2. Place potatoes in a large saucepan and cover with water. Bring to a boil; cook for 10-15 minutes or until
crisp-tender; drain. Toss with butter, salt and pepper.
3. Place tenderloin on a rack in a roasting pan. Pour marinade into saucepan; bring to a rolling boil. Boil for 1 minute; pour over meat. Arrange the potatoes around meat.
4. Cook, uncovered on Hi for 60-75 minutes, basting occasionally, or until beef reaches desired doneness. Slice; serve with pan juices and potatoes.

Beef Wellington
Makes 12 servings
Cook Time: 40 Min

Ingredients
1 (4 pound) beef tenderloin
2 (10.5 ounce) cans condensed beef consomme, undiluted
2 tablespoons tomato paste
1/2 teaspoon beef bouillon granules
2 tablespoons butter, softened
2 tablespoons all-purpose flour
1/2 cup Madeira wine
2 cups chopped fresh mushrooms
4 shallots, chopped
1/4 pound sliced deli ham, chopped
1/4 cup minced fresh parsley
1 (17.3 ounce) package frozen puff pastry sheets, thawed
2 tablespoons milk

Directions
1. Place the tenderloin in a greased baking pan; fold in ends of meat. Cook, uncovered, on Hi for 20-25 minutes or until browned. Cover and refrigerate for at least 2 hours or until chilled.
2. For sauce, in a large saucepan, combine the consomme, tomato paste and bouillon granules. Bring to a boil. Reduce heat; simmer, uncovered, for 20 minutes or until reduced to 2 cups. Combine butter and flour. Stir into sauce, a teaspoon at a time. Bring to a boil; cook and stir for 2 minutes or until thickened. Remove from the heat; stir in wine and set aside.
3. For the filling, in a large skillet, combine the mushrooms, shallots, ham and 2 tablespoons Madeira sauce. Cook over low heat for 10 minutes longer or until liquid has evaporated, stirring occasionally. Set aside.
4. On a lightly floured surface, unfold one puff pastry sheet; cut lengthwise along one fold line, forming two rectangles. Cut smaller rectangle into a 6-in. x 3-in. rectangle; use remaining piece for decorations if desired. Moisten a 6-in. edge of large rectangle with water. Attach smaller rectangle along that edge, pressing lightly to seal. Transfer to an ungreased baking sheet.
5. Spread half of the filling down the center of pastry. Place the tenderloin on the filling. Spread the remaining filling over the top of meat. Roll out remaining puff pastry into a rectangle 8 in. wide and 5 in. longer that the tenderloin; place over the meat. Brush pastry edges with milk; fold edges under meat.
6. Bake, uncovered, on Hi for 40 minutes (meat will be medium); cover lightly with foil if needed. Transfer to a serving platter. Let stand for 15 minutes before slicing. Re warm Madeira sauce if necessary. Serve with tenderloin.

Beef-Stuffed Potatoes
Makes 6 servings
Cook Time: 1 Hr 10 Min

Ingredients
6 medium baking potatoes
1 pound ground beef
2 tablespoons chopped onion
1/3 cup sour cream
1 (4 ounce) can chopped green chilies
3 tablespoons butter or margarine
1 tablespoon Worcestershire sauce
1 teaspoon salt
1/2 teaspoon garlic powder
1/2 teaspoon chili powder
3/4 cup shredded Cheddar cheese

Directions
1. Bake potatoes on Hi for 1 hour or until tender. Cool. Meanwhile, in a large skillet, cook the beef and onion over medium heat until the meat is no longer pink; drain.
2. Cut a thin slice off the top of each potato. Carefully scoop out pulp, leaving a thin shell; place pulp in a bowl. Add sour cream, chilies, butter, Worcestershire sauce, salt, garlic powder and chili powder; mash or beat.
3. Stir in meat mixture until combined. Stuff into potato shells.
4. Place on an ungreased baking sheet. Sprinkle with cheese. Bake on Hi for 10-15 minutes or until heated through.

Blue Cheese Beef Tenderloin
Makes 8 servings
Cook Time: 1 Hr

Ingredients
1 (3 pound) whole beef tenderloin
1/2 cup teriyaki sauce
1/2 cup red wine
2 cloves garlic, chopped
4 ounces blue cheese, crumbled
1/3 cup mayonnaise
2/3 cup sour cream
1 1/2 teaspoons Worcestershire sauce

Directions
1. Place beef in a shallow dish. Combine teriyaki sauce, red wine and garlic; pour over beef. Allow beef to marinate in refrigerator for 30 minutes.
2. Place tenderloin on pan and cook on Hi to desired doneness. Allow to set for 10 minutes before slicing.

3. In a saucepan over low heat, combine blue cheese, mayonnaise, sour cream and Worcestershire sauce. Stir until smooth; serve over sliced tenderloin.

Blue Cheese Burgers
Makes 4 servings

Ingredients
1 pound 80/20 ground beef
1/2 teaspoon garlic powder
1/2 teaspoon onion powder
1/2 cup blue cheese or favorite cheese
Salt and pepper to taste
4 buns

Directions
1. Mix ground beef and seasoning.
2. Form into balls and poke finger in the middle. Add cheese and pinch closed.
3. Place on 4-inch rack and cook on hi for 6-7 minutes.

Boneless Rump Roast
Makes 6 servings

Ingredients
4-5 pound boneless rump roast
4-6 cloves whole garlic
1 teaspoon fresh cracked peppercorns
1 large onion cut in slices
4 large russet potatoes cut, quartered
3 carrots peeled, cut, sticks
1/2 cup dry red wine (optional)
1/2 cup beef broth

Directions
1. Make small slits in the top of the roast and insert with garlic.
2. Place sliced onions on the 1-inch rack. Place roast on the onions, garlic side down.
3. Cook for 20 minutes on hi per pound.
4. Flip roast half way through, place carrots and potatoes around the roast.
5. Pour red wine and beef broth over roast, continue to cook.
6. Let meat rest for 10 minutes before slicing.

Cheeseburgers
Makes 4 servings

Ingredients
1 pound lean ground beef (may substitute 1/2 lb of ground beef with ground turkey)
1 tablespoon Worcestershire sauce
1 egg
1/2 cup dry bread crumbs
1/2 package dry onion soup mix
4 hamburger buns
4 slices of American cheese
Ketchup (optional)
Mustard (optional)
Sliced Onions (optional)
Pickle slices (optional)

Directions
1. Place ground beef in large mixing bowl. Add Worcestershire, egg, bread crumbs, onion soup and mix.
2. Divide mixture into four amounts and form into patties. Place patties on 4 inch rack. Cook on HI for 3-4 minutes per side. Place cheese on each burger and cook for one minute.

Corned Beef and Cabbage
Makes 8 servings
Cook Time: 4 Hrs

Ingredients
1 (5 1/2 pound) corned beef brisket
2 tablespoons pickling spice
1 large orange, sliced in rounds
2 stalks celery, sliced
1 large onion, sliced
1/2 cup cold water
6 tablespoons margarine, divided
1 large head cabbage, cored and sliced
1 cup Golden Delicious apples, cored and quartered with peel
1/4 cup cold water

Directions
1. Line a roasting pan with aluminum foil, leaving enough extra extending over the sides to cover and seal in the roast.
2. Rinse the brisket, and pat dry. Rub with pickling spice, and place in the prepared roasting pan. Arrange celery, orange and onion slices on and around the roast.
3. Pour in 1/2 cup of water, and wrap aluminum foil up over the roast tightly, making sure the ends are sealed.

4. Bake for about 4 hours on Hi or until meat is tender. About 45 minutes before the roasts time is up, heat 3 tablespoons of margarine and 1/4 cup of water in a large pot.
5. Add cabbage and apples, cover, and simmer over low heat for about 30 minutes. Occasionally shake the pot so that nothing sticks to the bottom. Serve with remaining margarine and sliced corned beef.

Corned Beef Mac and Cheese
Makes 6 servings

Ingredients
1 (12 ounce) can corned beef, crumbled
1 2/3 cups macaroni (cooked and drained)
1 1/2 cups cheddar cheese, grated
1 1/4 cups milk
1 (10 1/4 ounce) can condensed cream of chicken soup
1/2 cup chopped potato
2 teaspoons garlic (minced)
2 teaspoons onion powder
1 teaspoon italian seasoning
3/4 cup Italian seasoned breadcrumbs
1/4 margarine, cut up and added to the top

Directions
1. Mix together all ingredients except for the crumbs. Put into a greased 1 1/2 QT casserole dish (round).
2. Top with the buttered crumbs and bake on high for 20-25 minutes covered for 15 -20 minutes. Brown the top the last 5 to 10 minutes. until bubbly and lightly browned.

Country Fried Steak
Makes 4 servings

Ingredients
1/2 cup Bisquick mix
1/2 cup buttermilk
1/2 cup Progresso® garlic-herb bread crumbs
4 beef cube steaks (4 oz each)
1/3 cup canola or vegetable oil
1 cup thinly sliced onions
3-4 tablespoons Bisquick mix
1 cup skim milk
2 tablespoons chopped fresh parsley or 1 1/2 teaspoons dried parsley

Directions
1. Place sliced onions on the one inch rack and cook them on high for 8 minutes. In shallow dish, place 1/2 cup Bisquick.
2. In a small bowl, pour buttermilk. In another dish, place bread crumbs. Coat beef steaks with Bisquick. Dip each coated steak into buttermilk, then coat with bread crumbs.
3. Place on the 4-inch rack and cook for 8-9 minutes per side. In covered container, shake 3 tablespoons Bisquick and half-and-half until blended.
4. Pour liquid and onions into a 2 quart sauce pan. Cook over low heat 2 to 3 minutes, stirring occasionally until thickened.

Cuban Hamburgers
Makes 8 servings

Ingredients
1/2 lb ground beef
1 spanish chorizo, sausage ground up
1/2 lb ground pork
1 tablespoon ketchup
1/2 cup breadcrumbs (plain or italian seasoned for a kick of flavor)
1 egg, beaten
1 medium onion, chopped
3 fresh mashed garlic cloves
1 pinch ground cumin
salt & pepper, cooked patties

Directions
1. Mix all ingredients and form into patties. Cook on the 1 inch rack on HI for 5 -8 minutes depending on how cooked you like it.
2. Serve on a hamburger bun. Makes four quarter pounders or six to eight standard patties.

Enchilada Casserole
Makes 4 servings

Ingredients
1 1/2 lbs ground beef
1 small onion
4 flour tortillas
12 ounces olives
1 (12 ounce) can refried beans
12 ounces enchilada sauce
1 1/2 cups cheese

Directions
1. Brown meat with onion and seasonings. Drain grease. Layer each tortilla with beans, meat, spoonful of sauce, a couple olives and cheese.
2. Roll tortillas and lay seam side down on liner pan. Pour Remaining sauce and olives on top. Bake 25-30 minutes on Hi.
3. Place remaining cheese on top the last 2 minutes.

Glazed Beef Loaf
Makes 8 servings
Cook Time: 1 Hr 30 Min

Ingredients
2/3 cup milk
2 eggs
3 slices bread, cubed
1 1/2 cups shredded Cheddar cheese
2/3 cup shredded carrot
2/3 cup finely chopped onion
2 teaspoons salt
1/4 teaspoon pepper
2 pounds lean ground beef
1/4 cup packed brown sugar
1/4 cup ketchup
1 tablespoon prepared mustard

Directions
1. In a bowl combine milk, eggs and bread; let stand for 5 minutes. Add the cheese, carrot, onion, salt and pepper.
2. Crumble beef over mixture and mix well. Shape into a loaf in a greased baking dish. Bake, uncovered, on Hi 1-1/4 hours; drain.
3. Combine brown sugar, ketchup and mustard; spread over meat loaf. Bake 15 minutes longer or until the meat is no longer pink and a meat thermometer reads 160 degrees F.

Glazed Corned Beef
Makes 12 servings
Cook Time: 25 Min

Ingredients
1 (3 pound) corned beef brisket, trimmed
1 medium onion, sliced
1 celery rib, sliced
1/4 cup butter
1 cup packed brown sugar
2/3 cup ketchup
1/3 cup white vinegar
2 tablespoons prepared mustard
2 teaspoons prepared horseradish

Directions
1. Place corned beef and contents of seasoning packet in a dutch oven; cover with water. Add onion and celery.
2. Bring to a boil. Reduce heat; cover and simmer for 2-1/2 hours or until meat is tender. Drain and discard liquid and vegetables. Place beef on a rack in a shallow roasting pan; set aside.
3. In a saucepan, melt butter over medium heat. Stir in the remaining ingredients. Cook and stir until sugar is dissolved.
4. Brush over beef. Cook uncovered on Hi for 25 minutes. Let stand for 10 minutes before slicing.

Hamburger Pie
Makes 6 servings

Ingredients
1 1/2 lbs ground beef
1 (16 ounce) can green beans
1 (10 1/2 ounce) can tomato soup
1 medium onion, chopped
1 1/2 cups mashed potatoes (may substitute 1 small can biscuits)
1 cup of shredded cheddar cheese

Directions
1. Brown ground beef, drain. Add green beans, onions and tomato soup. Cover and simmer 10 minutes.
2. Pour mixture in a 2 quart baking dish, spoon mashed potatoes to top and top with cheese - bake on Hi for 18 minutes.
3. You may substitute mash potatoes with a can of biscuits - separate biscuits - cut in quarters place on top of burger mixture and sprinkle with cheese , bake on Hi for 17 to 19 minutes or until cheese is melted and biscuits are brown. Let stand 5 minutes.

Herbed Beef Rib Roast
Makes 10 servings
Cook Time: 2 Hrs 45 Min

Ingredients
1 tablespoon garlic powder
1 tablespoon ground mustard
1 teaspoon salt
1 teaspoon pepper
1 (6 pound) beef rib roast
1/4 cup water
1/4 cup beef broth
1 tablespoon red wine vinegar or cider vinegar

Directions
1. Combine the garlic powder, mustard, salt and pepper; rub over entire roast. Place roast fat side up in a shallow roasting pan.
2. Pour water, broth and vinegar into pan. Bake, uncovered, on Hi for 2-3/4 to 3 hours, basting frequently with pan juices, or until meat reaches desired doneness. Let stand for 10-15 minutes before slicing.

Herbed Beef Tenderloin
Makes 12 servings
Cook Time: 40 Min

Ingredients
1 (3 pound) whole beef tenderloin, trimmed
2 teaspoons olive or canola oil
2 garlic cloves, minced
1 1/2 teaspoons dried basil
1 1/2 teaspoons dried rosemary, crushed
1 teaspoon salt
1 teaspoon pepper

Directions
1. Tie tenderloin at 2-in. intervals with kitchen string. Combine oil and garlic; brush over meat. Combine the basil, rosemary, salt and pepper; sprinkle evenly over meat.
2. Place on a rack in a shallow roasting pan. Bake, uncovered on Hi for 40-50 minutes or until meat reaches desired doneness. Let stand for 10 minutes before slicing.

Lamb Chops With Feta
Makes 4 servings

Ingredients
2 tablespoons olive oil
1 garlic clove
1 tablespoon lemon juice
4 lamb chops, 1-inch thick
4 ounces feta cheese, crumbled
1/4 cup chopped ripe tomato
4 -6 pitted kalamata olives
1 tablespoon chopped parsley
salt and pepper

Directions
1. In a shallow dish, mix olive oil, garlic and lemon juice. Add the lamb chops and turn to coat on all sides.
2. Place inrefrigerator for 15 minutes. In small bowl mix feta, tomatoes, olives, and parsley. Set aside. Place lamb chops directly on 4" rack, sprinkle with salt and pepper.
3. Cook HI until done to taste, approximately 12-14 minutes (turning over 1/2 way). When chops are done, spoon equal portion of feta mixture on each chop and cook on HI until cheese melts.

Lasagna
Makes 6 servings

Ingredients
1 box of no-bake lasagna noodles (blue box)
1-1/2 pounds of ground beef, browned, drain fat
2 jars ready made marinara sauce (red sauce)
1 16-ounce container ricotta cheese
1 egg
1 tablespoon dried parsley
16 ounces of mozzarella cheese

Directions
1. Brown ground beef, season with salt and pepper. Add both jars of sauce and mix well. Cool for 10 minutes.
2. Mix cheese, egg and parsley until fluffy.
3. Grate cheese or use bag
4. Layering; place small amount of sauce, noodles, sauce, noodles, ricotta cheese (all) noodles, sauce and top with cheese. Let sit on counter for 20 minutes.
5. Bake on 1 inch rack for 25-27 minutes on Hi.
6. Let cool and allow setting for 10 minutes before serving.

Liver and Onions
Makes 4 servings

Ingredients
1 pound of 1/2 inch thick calf's liver
1/2 cup milk
1/2 teaspoon salt
1/2 teaspoon pepper
1/2 teaspoon seasoned salt
1 large onion sliced into rings
6 slices of bacon cut into small pieces

Directions
1. In a medium container marinate the liver in 1/2 cup milk and add spices. Let sit for up to one hour.
2. Slice onions and place on the 4 inch rack. Drain liver and place on top of onion rings.
3. Cut bacon into small pieces and place half on top of liver. Cook for 8 minutes and turn on power level high if liver is thicker than 1/2 inch cook for additional 2-3 minutes.
4. Place remaining bacon on liver and cook another 8 minutes. (If thicker add 2-3 minutes) Bacon will be nice and crisp. 5. Let liver sit for 5 minutes with dome on.

Meatloaf
Makes 4 servings

Ingredients
1 pound extra-lean ground beef
1 large egg, lightly beaten
1/2 cup ketchup
1/4 cup grated onion
1/4 cup breadcrumbs
1 teaspoon Worcestershire sauce
1 tablespoon minced fresh parsley
1 teaspoon minced fresh thyme
1/4 teaspoon kosher salt
1/4 teaspoon black pepper
1/4 teaspoon garlic powder

Directions
1. Combine the beef, egg, ketchup, onion, breadcrumbs, Worcestershire sauce and all herbs and spices in a large bowl.
2. Use your hands to mix everything together. Place on 1 inch rack and cook on power level high for 22-24 minutes. Let rest for 5 minutes to cool before slicing.

Meatloaf Roll
Makes 4 servings

Ingredients
2 slices white bread or 2 slices whole wheat bread
1 1/2 lbs ground meat
1 medium onion, minced
1/4 cup milk
1 teaspoon salt
1 dash Worcestershire sauce
1/4 teaspoon pepper
1 dash seasoning salt
1 (8 ounce) package sliced pepperoni or 1 (8 ounce) package ham or 1 (8 ounce) package salami
1 (10 ounce) package frozen chopped spinach, cooked and drained
4 ounces favorite shredded cheese

Directions
1. About 1 1/2 hours before preparing: Into medium bowl, tear bread into small pieces (You can also lightly toast in toaster or place in Nu-Wave for 2-4 minutes).
2. Add meat, onion and seasonings. Mix well but do not over mix. On waxed paper or saran wrap, pat meat mixture into 12X8 inch rectangle. On meat rectangle, arrange sliced meat to cover meatloaf mixture; top with spinach and cheese.
3. Starting at narrow end, roll meat mixture, jellyroll fashion, lifting waxed paper to help shape roll. Seal sides so cheese does not get out. Place rolled loaf, seam side down, in meatloaf pan.
4. Bake on 1" rack for 45-50 minutes on power 6 or 30 minutes on high. When meat starts to brown, cover loosely with a tent of foil to prevent over browning.

Peppered Beef Tenderloin
Makes 10 servings
Cook Time: 45 Min

Ingredients
3 tablespoons coarsely ground pepper
2 tablespoons olive oil
1 tablespoon grated lemon peel
1 teaspoon salt
2 garlic cloves, minced
1 (3 pound) whole beef tenderloin

Directions
1. Combine the pepper, oil, lemon peel, salt and garlic; rub over tenderloin. Place on a greased rack in a foil-lined roasting pan.

2. Bake, uncovered, on Hi for 45-65 minutes or until beef reaches desired doneness. Cover and let stand for 10 minutes before slicing.

Porterhouse Steaks
Makes 4 servings

Ingredients
1 (2 1/2 lb) porterhouse steaks (2-inch-thick)
1 teaspoon salt, plus additional for sprinkling (preferably sea salt)
1 tablespoon olive oil, for drizzling

Directions
1. Pat steaks dry and rub all over with 1 teaspoon salt. Cook steaks on Hi for about 9 minutes per side.
2. To serve steaks transfer steaks to a cutting board and let stand, uncovered, 10 minutes.
3. Cut each section of meat off bone, then slice each piece crosswise against the grain and arrange slices on a platter. Sprinkle lightly with salt and drizzle with oil.

Pot Roast
Makes 6 servings

Ingredients
2 1/2 to 3 pound Chuck or shoulder roast
1/4 cup flour
3 large potatoes, cleaned and peeled into quarters
4 large carrots cut on the bias
1 large onion cut in wedges
3-4 cloves garlic, peeled
1 teaspoon black pepper
1/2 cup red wine
1 teaspoon pepper
1 teaspoon salt
1 tablespoon soy sauce
1 tablespoon Worcestershire sauce

Directions
1. Place all the vegetables in a cooking bag. Place meat on the vegetables and season with wine, soy sauce, salt and pepper.
2. Tie bag and Cook on Hi for 20 min per pound.

Reuben Sandwich

Ingredients
4 tablespoons butter
2 slices rye bread
1 ounce thinly sliced corned beef
1/4 cup sauerkraut, squeezed dry
1 slice swiss cheese or 1 slice gruyere cheese
1 tablespoon thousand island dressing

Directions
1. Lightly butter one side of each slice of bread. On the unbuttered side, place corned beef, sauerkraut, and cheese. Spread with dressing.
2. Top with second slice of bread, buttered side up. Place directly on 4" rack and Nu-Wave on HI for 7 minutes or until the top is lightly toasted and the cheese is melted.
3. Place directly on the 4" rack and Nu-Wave on HI for 4 minutes or until well heated and cheese melts.

Short Ribs
Makes 4 servings

Ingredients
4 pounds short ribs, cut between the bones, then cut into 3-inch lengths
3/4 cup Hoisin sauce
2 cups red wine-dry
2 tablespoons chopped garlic

Directions
1. Place rib, Hoisin, wine and garlic in large bowl. Cover and let marinate overnight in the refrigerator.
2. Remove short ribs from marinade and set aside. Bring marinade to boil with 3 cups of water in a heavy pot large enough to hold one layer of short ribs.
3. Add ribs and 1/2 teaspoon of whole peppercorns. Simmer for one hour. Take out and reserve 1 cup of liquid. Place ribs on 4 inch rack and baste with reserve liquid. Cook for 4 minutes per side.
4. Let ribs sit with dome on for 2-3 minutes. Serve over rice.

Steak and Lobster Tails
Makes 2 servings

Ingredients
2 rib-eye steaks (6-8 ounces)
1 tablespoon olive oil
1/2 teaspoon black pepper
2 4-5 ounce lobster tails
3 tablespoons butter
1 teaspoon fresh parsley

Directions
1. Brush steaks with olive oil and sprinkle with pepper (no salt, dries steak out) Place on 4-inch rack and cook 1- inch steaks for 6-7 minutes per side for medium rare.
2. When you turn steak add lobster tails and cook for 6-7 minutes. 2. Remove steak and let rest for 5 minutes.
3. In the mean time, place butter in oven safe dish and melt for 1-2 minutes, leaving lobster on the 4-inch rack. When lobster and butter are done, steak will be rested. Meal will be ready.

Steak with Peppercorns
Makes 4 servings

Ingredients
1-1/4 pounds of top sirloin steak (about 1 inch thick)
1-1/2 teaspoons of chopped rosemary
2-1/2 teaspoons of olive oil, divided
1 cup pomegranate juice
4 teaspoons of (packed) golden brown sugar
2 teaspoons of balsamic vinegar
4 cups of arugula washed and dried.

Directions
1. Sprinkle steak very generously with peppercorn Mélange coarsely grinded. Sprinkle each side of steak with half of chopped rosemary.
2. Place steak on 4 inch grill and cook to desired doneness, 6-7 minutes per side for medium-rare, 7-8 minutes per side for medium and 9-10 minutes for well-done. (Thawed) Frozen see cooking chart.
3. Place pomegranate juice, golden brown sugar, and vinegar to sauté pan and boil till reduced to a scant ¼ cup of glaze. Adjust seasonings.
4. Toss arugula and remaining olive oil and balsamic vinegar.
5. Slice steak and serve on arugula.

Tortilla Beef Bake

Makes 6 servings
Cook Time: 30 Min

Ingredients

1 1/2 pounds ground beef
1 (10.75 ounce) can condensed cream of chicken soup, undiluted
2 1/2 cups crushed tortilla chips, divided
1 (16 ounce) jar salsa
1 1/2 cups shredded Cheddar cheese

Directions

1. In a skillet, cook beef over medium heat until no longer pink; drain. Stir in soup. Sprinkle 1-1/2 cups tortilla chips in a greased shallow 2-1/2-qt. baking dish. Top with beef mixture, salsa and cheese.
2. Bake on Hi for 25-30 minutes or until bubbly. Sprinkle with the remaining chips. Bake 3 minutes longer or until chips are lightly toasted.

Breakfast

through. Cut popover into quarters; serve with apple topping.

Apple Bread
Makes 10 servings
Cook Time: 1 Hr

Ingredients
1/2 cup butter
1 cup sugar
2 eggs
2 cups all-purpose flour
1 teaspoon baking soda
1/2 teaspoon salt
1 teaspoon ground cinnamon
1/2 teaspoon ground cloves
2 apples - peeled, cored and chopped

Directions
1. Lightly grease a loaf pan.
2. In a bowl, mix the butter and sugar until smooth and creamy. Beat in the eggs.
3. In a separate bowl, sift together the flour, baking soda, salt, cinnamon, and cloves. Mix into the butter mixture until moistened. Fold in the apples. Transfer to the prepared loaf pan.
4. Bake 1 hour on Hi until a toothpick inserted in the center comes out clean. Cool in the pan for 15 minutes before removing to a wire rack to cool completely.

Apple Popover
Makes 4 servings
Cook Time: 20 Min

Ingredients
4 egg whites
1/2 cup fat-free milk
1/2 cup all-purpose flour
1 tablespoon butter or stick margarine, melted
1/8 teaspoon salt
1 1/2 cups finely chopped peeled apple
1/2 cup apple jelly
2 tablespoons water
1/8 teaspoon ground cinnamon

Directions
1. In a mixing bowl, beat the egg whites, milk, flour, butter and salt until smooth. Pour into a square baking dish coated with nonstick cooking spray.
2. Bake on Hi for 20-25 minutes or until golden and puffed. Meanwhile, in a small saucepan, combine the apples, jelly, water and cinnamon. heat over low heat until jelly is melted and mixture is heated

Apple Pancake
Makes 2 servings

Ingredients
2 tablespoons margarine or butter
2 large eggs
1/2 cup all purpose flour
1/2 cup milk
1/4 teaspoon salt
2 Tbsp packed brown sugar
1/4 tsp ground cinnamon
1 apple, peeled and sliced
Lemon juice and powdered sugar (optional)

Directions
1. Beat eggs lightly in med bowl with wire whisk or hand beater. Beat in flour, milk, and salt just until mixed. Melt butter in pie plate.
2. Brush around pie plate to distribute evenly. Sprinkle brown sugar and ground cinnamon evenly over the melted butter. Arrange sliced apples over the sugar.
3. Pour batter over apple. Bake on Hi for 30-35 minutes. Quickly loosen the edge of pancake and turn upside down onto a serving plate. Serve with powdered sugar and lemon juice on the side.

Bacon Cake
Makes 8 servings
Cook Time: 30 Min

Ingredients
12 slices bacon
1/4 cup packed brown sugar
1 (9 ounce) package white cake mix, batter prepared as directed on package
1 teaspoon maple flavored extract
1/4 cup maple syrup

Directions
1. Grease a round cake pan.
2. Place the bacon in a large, deep skillet; cook over medium-high heat, turning occasionally, until lightly browned but still soft, about 7 minutes. Drain the bacon slices on a paper towel-lined plate.
3. Place the bacon on the bottom of the greased cake pan, overlapping slices as necessary to fit. Sprinkle the bacon strips with the brown sugar.
4. Combine the prepared cake batter, maple extract, and maple syrup in a large bowl, mixing well. Pour the batter over the brown sugar and bacon in the cake pan.

5. Bake on Hi for 15-20 minutes or until a toothpick inserted in the center comes out clean. Cool cake slightly and remove from pan by inverting onto a serving platter. Cut into wedges to serve.

Banana Pumpkin Bread
Makes 8 servings

Ingredients
1 (18 ounce) box yellow cake mix
2 eggs
3 bananas
1 cup milk
1 teaspoon cinnamon
1 teaspoon nutmeg
1/2 cup oil

Directions
1. Mash the bananas.
2. Add the slightly beaten eggs, milk, cinnamon, oil, and nutmeg and mix well.
3. Add the cake mix half at a time making sure all mix is incorporated before adding the second batch.
4. Add 2 cups of pumpkin if wanting pumpkin bread. Fill loaf pans 2/3 full.
5. Bake on Hi for 12 minutes uncovered. The crust will form on top but it will not be done in the middle.
6. Put a little butter over the top. Cover with tin foil allowing room for the bread to rise. Bake another 12 minutes on full power. Butter and tinfoil are essential for the last baking to prevent cracking.

Biscuit Sandwiches
Makes 6 servings
Cook Time: 12 Min

Ingredients
1 1/2 cups all-purpose flour
1 tablespoon baking powder
1 tablespoon sugar
1 teaspoon salt
1/4 cup shortening
3/4 cup milk
6 eggs
1 tablespoon butter or margarine
6 slices process American cheese
6 slices fully cooked ham

Directions
1. In a bowl, combine dry ingredients; cut in shortening until crumbly. stir in milk just until moistened. turn onto a lightly floured surface; knead five to six times. Roll to 1/2-in. thickness; cut with a 2-3/4-in. biscuit cutter. Place on an ungreased baking sheet. Bake on Hi for 12-15 minutes or until light golden brown; cool slightly. In a skillet over medium heat, fry eggs in butter until completely set. Split the biscuits; place cheese, hot eggs and ham on bottoms. Replace tops. Serve immediately.

Biscuits
Makes 3 servings

Ingredients
6 biscuits (Pillsbury Southern Style)
2 ounces butter

Directions
1. Place 6 Pillsbury southern style Biscuits in your Nuwave. Place on 4 inch rack.
2. Bake on HI for 12 minutes for golden brown.

Blueberry-Sausage Breakfast Cake
Makes 9 servings
Cook Time: 35 Min

Ingredients
1/2 cup butter, softened
3/4 cup sugar
1/4 cup packed brown sugar
2 eggs
2 cups all-purpose flour
1 teaspoon baking powder
1/2 teaspoon baking soda
1 cup sour cream
1 pound bulk pork sausage, cooked and drained
1 cup fresh or frozen blueberries
1/2 cup chopped pecans
1/2 cup sugar
2 tablespoons cornstarch
1/2 cup water
2 cups fresh or frozen blueberries

Directions
1. In a mixing bowl, cream butter and sugars. Add eggs, one at a time, beating well after each addition.
2. Combine flour, baking powder and baking soda; add alternately with sour cream to creamed mixture, beating well after each addition. Fold in sausage and blueberries.
3. Pour into a greased baking pan. Sprinkle with pecans. Bake at on Hi for 35-40 minutes or until cake tests done.
4. For sauce, combine sugar and cornstarch in a saucepan. Add water and blueberries. Cook and stir until thick and bubbly. Spoon over individual servings.

Breakfast Bars

Makes 24 servings
Cook Time: 30 Min

Ingredients
1 cup butter or margarine, softened
1 cup packed brown sugar
1 cup quick-cooking oats
1 cup all-purpose flour
1 cup whole wheat flour
1/2 cup toasted wheat germ
4 eggs
2 cups chopped pecans
1 cup flaked coconut
1 cup semisweet chocolate chips

Directions
1. In a mixing bowl, cream the butter and brown sugar. Combine oats, flours and wheat germ; gradually add to creamed mixture.
2. Press into a greased baking pan. In a small bowl, beat eggs until foamy. Stir in pecans, coconut and chocolate chips. Spread evenly over crust.
3. Bake on Hi for 30-35 minutes or until edges are golden brown. Cool on a wire rack. Cut into bars. Store in the refrigerator.

Breakfast Buns

Makes 16 servings
Cook Time: 20 Min

Ingredients
2 cups all-purpose flour
3/4 cup sugar, divided
1 tablespoon baking powder
3 tablespoons butter or margarine
2 eggs, lightly beaten
1 teaspoon vanilla extract
1/2 cup milk
1 cup raisins
1/2 teaspoon ground cinnamon

Directions
1. In a mixing bowl, stir together flour, 1/2 cup sugar and baking powder; cut in butter. Combine eggs, vanilla and milk; add to dry ingredients and stir just until moistened.
2. Add raisins. Drop by tablespoonfuls onto greased baking sheet. Combine the cinnamon and remaining sugar; sprinkle over buns. Bake on Hi for 20-25 minutes or until light golden brown. Serve warm.

Breakfast in a Muffin

Makes 12 servings
Cook Time: 15 Min

Ingredients
1 cup whole wheat flour
1 cup all-purpose flour
1/4 cup sugar
4 teaspoons baking powder
1/4 teaspoon salt
1 cup milk
1/4 cup vegetable oil
2 eggs, divided
1 (8 ounce) package cream cheese, softened
1/4 cup shredded Cheddar cheese
1/4 teaspoon seasoned salt
4 bacon strips, cooked and crumbled

Directions
1. In a large bowl, combine first five ingredients. Combine milk, oil and 1 egg; stir into dry ingredients just until moistened.
2. Fill greased or paper-lined muffin cups half full. In a mixing bowl, beat cream cheese and second egg.
3. Add cheddar cheese and seasoned salt; mix well. Stir in bacon. Spoon 2 tablespoons in the center of each muffin.
4. Bake on Hi for 15-20 minutes or until muffins test done. Serve warm.

Breakfast Pie
Makes 6 servings
Cook Time: 40 Min

Ingredients
8 bacon strips, diced
1/4 cup crushed cornflakes
5 eggs, lightly beaten
1/2 cup milk
1/2 cup small curd cottage cheese
1 1/2 cups shredded Cheddar cheese
1 green onion, sliced
1/2 teaspoon salt
1/8 teaspoon pepper
2 1/2 cups frozen cubed hash brown potatoes

Directions
1. In a large skillet, cook bacon over medium heat until crisp. Remove to paper towels. Drain, reserving 2 teaspoons drippings.
2. Stir reserved drippings into cornflakes; set aside. in a bowl, combine the eggs, milk, cottage cheese, cheddar cheese, onion, salt and pepper until blended. Stir in hash browns.
3. Pour into a greased pie plate. Sprinkle with bacon and the cornflake mixture. Cover and refrigerate overnight.
4. Remove from the refrigerator 30 minutes before baking. Bake on Hi for 45-50 minutes or until a knife inserted near the center comes out clean. Let stand for 5-10 minutes before cutting.

Breakfast Pizza
Makes 6 servings
Cook Time: 10 Min

Ingredients
2 cups frozen shredded hash brown potatoes
1/4 teaspoon ground cumin
1/4 teaspoon chili powder
2 tablespoons canola oil, divided
1 cup egg substitute
2 tablespoons fat-free milk
1/4 teaspoon salt
2 green onions, chopped
2 tablespoons diced sweet red pepper
1 tablespoon finely chopped jalapeno pepper
1 garlic clove, minced
1 (16 ounce) package pre-baked Italian bread shell crust
1/2 cup salsa
3/4 cup shredded reduced-fat Cheddar cheese

Directions

1. In a nonstick skillet, cook hash browns, cumin and chili powder in 1 tablespoon oil over medium heat until golden.
2. Remove and keep warm. In a bowl, beat egg substitute, milk and salt; set aside. In the same skillet, sauté the onions, peppers and garlic in remaining oil until tender.
3. Add egg mixture. Cook and stir over medium heat until almost set. Remove from the heat.
4. Place crust on an ungreased pizza pan. Spread salsa over crust. Top with egg mixture. Sprinkle with hash browns and cheese. Bake on Hi for 8-10 minutes or until cheese is melted.

Breakfast Supreme
Makes 12 servings
Cook Time: 35 Min

Ingredients
1 pound bulk pork sausage
1 pound ground beef
1 small onion, chopped
3/4 cup sliced fresh mushrooms
1/2 cup chopped green pepper
1 teaspoon salt
1/4 teaspoon pepper
2 tablespoons butter or margarine, melted
2 cups shredded Cheddar cheese, divided
12 eggs
2/3 cup whipping cream

Directions
1. In a large skillet, cook the sausage, beef, onion, mushrooms and green pepper over medium heat until meat is no longer pink; drain. Stir in salt and pepper; set aside.
2. Pour butter into an ungreased baking dish. sprinkle with 1 cup cheese. beat eggs; pour over cheese. Top with sausage mixture. Pour the cream over sausage mixture. Sprinkle with remaining cheese. Cover and refrigerate for 8 hours or overnight.
3. Remove from the refrigerator 30 minutes before baking. Bake, uncovered, on Hi for 35-40 minutes or until set. Let stand for 10 minutes before cutting.

Breakfast Tart

Makes 20 servings
Cook Time: 40 Min

Ingredients
4 cups all-purpose flour
1 tablespoon white sugar
1 teaspoon baking powder
2 teaspoons salt
1 3/4 cups shortening
1/2 cup cold water
1 egg
1 tablespoon vinegar
8 slices bacon
1 tablespoon butter
1/2 cup chopped onion
1/3 cup finely diced smoked ham
3 cups heavy cream
8 eggs, beaten
1/4 teaspoon salt
1/2 teaspoon freshly ground black pepper
1/4 teaspoon nutmeg
3 tablespoons finely chopped fresh basil
1 tablespoon fresh thyme, minced
1 (3 ounce) package cream cheese, diced
1/2 cup shredded Cheddar cheese
1/2 cup shredded Monterey Jack cheese
1 bunch green onions, chopped
1/3 cup sliced almonds

Directions
1. Mix together flour, sugar, baking powder and salt. Cut in shortening until mixture resembles coarse crumbs. Add water, egg, and vinegar. Mix together but do not work too much. Divide pastry into two pieces, cover and chill for 30 minutes.
2. Form each piece into a round and roll out crust on lightly floured surface. Carefully fit into two 10 inch tart pans.
3. Blind bake tart shells on Hi until golden brown. Let cool.
4. Place bacon in a large, deep skillet. Cook over medium high heat until evenly brown. Drain, crumble, and set aside.
5. Saute onion in butter until translucent. Divide ham, bacon and onion into two equal portions and sprinkle over the bottom of tart shells.
6. Whisk together cream and beaten eggs. Add salt, pepper, nutmeg, basil, and thyme, and stir well. Pour egg mixture over bacon mixture. Sprinkle cream cheese cubes and grated Cheddar and Monterey Jack cheeses over the top of each filled tart. Sprinkle green onions over cheese, followed by sliced almonds.
7. Bake on Hi for 30 to 40 minutes. Let cool slightly, then cut and serve.

Cheddar Biscuits

Makes 12 servings

Ingredients
2 cups Bisquick
3/4 cup 1% fat buttermilk (or low-fat)
1 cup cheddar cheese, shredded
2 tablespoons margarine or 2 tablespoons butter
1/4 teaspoon garlic powder
1/4 teaspoon dried parsley flakes, crushed fine

Directions
1. Combine the baking mix, milk and cheddar cheese in a medium bowl.
2. Mix by hand until well combined. Divide the dough into 12 equal portions (about 3 tbsp each) and spoon onto a lightly greased or nonstick cookie sheet.
3. Flatten each biscuit a bit with your fingers. 5 Bake in Nuwave for 8 -10 mins on 8 (or 80 percent heat). Until the tops of the biscuits begin to brown.
4. In a small bowl, combine the buttery spread with the garlic powder and the parsley flakes.
5. Heat this mixture for 30 seconds in the microwave, then brush a light coating over the top of each biscuit.

Corn Muffins

Makes 12 servings
Cook Time: 20 Min

Ingredients

3/4 cup cornmeal
1 1/2 cups all-purpose flour
1/2 teaspoon baking powder
1/2 teaspoon salt
1/2 cup butter
1/4 cup honey
2/3 cup white sugar
2 eggs
1/2 cup buttermilk
1 large ripe banana, cut into 1 inch slices
1/2 cup peanut butter

Directions

1. Grease muffin cups, or line with paper muffin liners. Combine cornmeal, flour, baking powder, and salt in a bowl.
2. Beat the butter, honey, and sugar with an electric mixer in a large bowl until light and fluffy. The mixture should be noticeably lighter in color.
3. Add the room-temperature eggs one at a time, allowing each egg to blend into the butter mixture before adding the next. Pour in the flour mixture alternately with the buttermilk, mixing until just incorporated.
4. Fill each muffin cup about 1/3 full. Place a banana slice onto the batter in each cup and top with about ½ teaspoon of peanut butter, pressing down slightly to cover the banana. Continue to fill each muffin cup with batter, until the cup is 2/3 full.
5. Bake on Hi until a toothpick inserted into the center comes out clean, 20 to 25 minutes. Cool in the pans for 10 minutes before removing to cool completely on a wire rack.

Easy Breakfast Nachos

Makes 4 servings
Cook Time: 20 Min

Ingredients

1 pound bulk chorizo sausage
1/2 onion, chopped
5 eggs, beaten
4 tomatoes, chopped
2 jalapeno peppers, sliced
1 (8 ounce) package tortilla chips
1 (8 ounce) package finely shredded Mexican blend cheese

Directions

1. Cook the chorizo in a skillet over medium heat until crumbled and evenly browned, about 5 minutes; drain and set aside.
2. Cook the onion in the same skillet until soft; stir in the eggs and scramble with the onion. Mix in the tomatoes and continue to cook and stir until eggs are nearly set; remove from heat.
3. Spread a layer of tortilla chips into a baking dish. Scatter the chorizo and the scrambled egg mixture over the chips. Top with jalapeno slices and cover with the cheese.
4. Bake on Hi until cheese is melted, 7 to 10 minutes.

Egg Omelette

Ingredients

2 eggs
1/8 cup water or 1/8 cup milk
2 slices of your favorite cheese
1/4 cup diced onion
1/4 cup diced green pepper
1/2 cup chopped ham or 1/2 cup cooked bacon
1 dash salt and pepper

Directions

1. Whisk eggs, salt & Pepper and milk or water in a small bowl.
2. Saute ham, onion and pepper in 10" non-stick baking pan.
3. Cook eggs in small circular dish for 10 minutes on Hi on 1" rack stir half way. When egg is cooked, place ham, onion and pepper inside of egg mixture, fold egg over omlette style.
4. Place cheese on top and put on 4" rack for 2-3 minutes until cheese is melted.

Egg White Muffin
Makes 2 servings

Ingredients
1 pita whole wheat
6 tablespoons hummus
2 mozzarella string cheese, pieces
1/4 cup monterey jack pepper cheese, grated
2 pieces Canadian bacon
1/4 cup egg white
1 tablespoon granulated garlic
1 tablespoon graunlated minced onion
1/4 teaspoon hot pepper flakes
1 dash pepper
1 dash paprika

Directions
1. Split Pita pocket in half. Cook your eggs 1 minute on hi in your microwave until it full "puffs up". Remove.
2. Add 2-3 tablespoons on hummus to each of the pita bread - spread hummus on the inside part of the pita and then add: string cheese and wait for eggs to be done.
3. Once egg is mostly done 3/4 (or 1 minutes in the Microwave) of the way done add to top of pita, top with Canadian bacon and top with pepper jack cheese. Cook for 3-4 minutes on hi.

English Muffins
Makes 12 servings

Ingredients
1 cup milk
3 tablespoons butter
1 egg
1/2 teaspoon salt
2 teaspoons sugar
3 cups all-purpose flour (or more)
1 1/2 teaspoons dry yeast
1/4 cup cornmeal, to dust on bottom of muffins

Directions
1. In your bread machine start the dough cycle. When the cycle is finished.
2. Sprinkle corn meal over your work area. Use your hands to pat the dough into a 1/2 inch thick.
3. Turn the dough so that each side gets lightly coated with cornmeal.
4. Cut into 8 to 10 rounds. An empty large tuna can works well When you run out of dough gather up the trimmings and cut more rounds.
5. Once dough as risen, place in Nuwave in round pan. Set the timer for 8 min on 8 temp.

French Breakfast Puffs
Makes 12 servings
Cook Time: 20 Min

Ingredients
1/3 cup shortening
1 cup sugar, divided
1 egg
1 1/2 cups all-purpose flour
1 1/2 teaspoons baking powder
1/2 teaspoon salt
1/4 teaspoon ground nutmeg
1/2 cup milk
1 teaspoon ground cinnamon
6 tablespoons butter, melted

Directions
1. In a small mixing bowl, beat shortening, 1/2 cup sugar and egg until smooth. Combine the flour, baking powder, salt and nutmeg; add to the sugar mixture alternately with milk.
2. Fill greased muffin cups two-thirds full. Bake on Hi for 20 minutes or until a toothpick inserted near the center comes out clean. Cool for 5 minutes before removing from pan.
3. Meanwhile, combine cinnamon and remaining sugar in a shallow bowl. Roll the warm puffs in butter, then in cinnamon-sugar. Serve immediately.

Ham Breakfast Braid
Makes 6 servings
Cook Time: 30 Min

Ingredients
1/2 cup milk
4 ounces cream cheese, softened
8 eggs
salt and pepper to taste
2 (8 ounce) packages refrigerated crescent roll dough
4 ounces cooked ham, thinly sliced
1 cup shredded Cheddar cheese

Directions
1. Beat milk and cream cheese together until smooth. Mix in eggs, and season with salt and pepper.
2. Heat a lightly oiled skillet over medium high heat and cook egg mixture until eggs are almost set. Arrange the crescent rolls from one package into a rectangle shape on top of a lightly greased cookie sheet.
3. Place rolls from remaining package along the edges of the two long sides of the rectangle, with the broad half of the rolls on top of the first layer of rolls, and the pointed ends extending over the sides of the pan.
4. Arrange the ham in a layer down the center of the dough. Spoon the cooked egg mixture on top of the ham and then sprinkle the cheddar cheese on top of the eggs.
5. Bring the corners of the rolls together over the cheese to form a 'braid' shape. Bake on Hi for 25 to 30 minutes, until cheese is melted and rolls are golden brown.

Hashbrown Breakfast Bake
Makes 10 servings
Cook Time: 50 Min

Ingredients
5 cups frozen shredded hashbrowns, thawed
3 cups cooked ham, chopped
1 green bell pepper, chopped
3 cups Mexican cheese blend, shredded
5 eggs
1 1/4 cups Daisy Brand Sour Cream
1 cup milk
1 teaspoon dried oregano
1 teaspoon salt
1/2 teaspoon chili powder
1/2 teaspoon onion powder
3/4 cup pico de gallo

Directions
1. Grease a baking dish or spray with cooking spray.
2. Mix the hashbrowns with the ham, bell pepper, and 2 cups cheese in a medium bowl. In another medium bowl, whisk together the eggs, 1 cup of sour cream, milk, oregano, salt, chili powder, and onion powder. Combine the hashbrown mixture with the egg mixture. Pour the mixture into the baking dish.
3. Bake on Hi for 35 minutes; remove the casserole from the oven and sprinkle with the remaining cheese.
4. Return the casserole to the nu wave and bake for 15 to 20 minutes or until the hash browns are tender and knife inserted in the center comes out clean. Top each slice of casserole with servings with Pico de Gallo and a dollop of sour cream.

Mini Breakfast Quiches
Makes 12 servings
Cook Time: 30 Min

Ingredients
24 (2 inch) frozen mini tart shells
6 slices bacon
6 eggs
1 1/2 cups heavy cream
1/4 cup all-purpose flour
2 teaspoons garlic salt
2 teaspoons onion powder
1 teaspoon chili powder
1/2 teaspoon ground cumin
2 cups shredded Cheddar cheese
1/2 cup diced green bell pepper
1/2 cup diced red bell pepper
1/2 cup cubed fully cooked ham
1/4 cup salsa
1/2 cup shredded Cheddar cheese

Directions
1. Place the tart shells into muffin pans and set aside. Cook the bacon in a large, deep skillet over medium-high heat, turning occasionally, until evenly browned, about 10 minutes. Drain on a paper towel-lined plate; crumble once cool.
2. Beat the eggs in a mixing bowl; whisk in the cream, flour, garlic salt, onion powder, chili powder, and cumin until smooth. Stir in the crumbled bacon, 2 cups Cheddar cheese, green bell pepper, red bell pepper, ham, and salsa.
3. Ladle the mixture into the tart shells; sprinkle with 1/2 cup of Cheddar cheese.
4. Bake on Hi until a knife inserted into the center of the quiche comes out clean, 20 to 25 minutes.

Monte Cristo
Makes 6 servings

Ingredients
20 slices sandwich bread
1 1/2 lbs sliced virginia ham
25 slices swiss cheese, deli sliced
1 cup milk
4 eggs
3 teaspoons Dijon mustard
1 pinch salt
1 pinch pepper

Directions
1. In large Casserole baking dish, layer bottom with bread, one piece at a time to fill bottom of pan.
2. Then add one layer of ham, when layer is complete add one slice of cheese until layer is complete. Repeat layers until casserole is up to casserole height (try to make sure last layer is with cheese.).
3. Mix together: milk, Dijon, eggs, salt and pepper. Once mixed well, add to top of Strata making sure it is covered evenly. If there is excess on top, let drain into middle and side. (You can help this process.)
4. The top will look soggy and the mixture will soak into the bread. The next morning, cook at HI for 10 minutes covered, then 1-15 minutes uncovered. 5 Serve with strawberry jam.

Oatmeal Breakfast Treats
Makes 15 servings
Cook Time: 15 Min

Ingredients
2 eggs
3/4 cup packed brown sugar
1/2 cup vegetable oil
1/4 cup evaporated milk
1 teaspoon vanilla extract
2 1/2 cups old-fashioned oats
1/2 cup whole wheat flour
1/2 cup all-purpose flour
1/2 teaspoon salt
3/4 cup raisins
1/2 cup chopped walnuts

Directions
1. In a mixing bowl, combine the first five ingredients; mix well. Combine oats, flours and salt; add to brown sugar mixture and mix well.
2.Stir in raisins and walnuts. Drop by rounded tablespoonfuls onto greased baking sheets. Bake on Hi for 12-14 minutes or until set.

Ooey Gooey Breakfast Rolls
Makes 16 servings
Cook Time: 30 Min

Ingredients
1/2 cup chopped pecans (optional)
1 (1 pound) loaf frozen bread dough, thawed
1/2 cup butter, melted
1/2 cup packed brown sugar
1 (3.5 ounce) package cook and serve butterscotch pudding mix
2 teaspoons ground cinnamon

Directions
1. Grease a Bundt pan, and sprinkle the pecans into the bottom of the pan.
2. Cut the thawed bread dough in half, and cut each half into 8 pieces. Roll the 16 dough pieces into balls, and place them into the pan on top of the nuts.
3. Mix the melted butter and brown sugar together in a bowl, and set aside. Sprinkle the butterscotch pudding mix over the rolls, then sprinkle on the cinnamon.
4. Pour the butter mixture over the rolls, cover the pan loosely with plastic wrap, refrigerate, and let the rolls rise for 6 to 8 hours, or overnight.
5. Remove the plastic wrap from the pan, and bake the rolls on Hi for 25 to 30 minutes, until golden brown.

Orange Breakfast Ring

Makes 16 servings
Cook Time: 15 Min

Ingredients

1 (8 ounce) package cream cheese, softened
1/2 cup sugar
1 tablespoon grated orange peel
2 (8 ounce) cans refrigerated crescent rolls
1/3 cup chopped almonds, toasted
1/2 cup confectioners' sugar
1 tablespoon orange juice
Sliced almonds

Directions

1. In a small mixing bowl, beat the cream cheese, sugar and orange peel until blended; set aside.
2. Unroll both tubes of dough; press perforations and seams together to form two rectangles. Overlap rectangles at one end and press the seam to seal. Spread cream cheese mixture over dough to within 1/2 in. of edges. Sprinkle with the chopped almonds.
3. Roll up jelly-roll style, starting with a long side; pinch seam to seal. Place seam side down on a greased baking sheet; pinch ends together to form a ring. With scissors, cut from outside edge two-thirds of the way toward center of ring at 1-in. intervals. Separate strips slightly; twist to allow filling to show.
4. Bake on Hi for 15-18 minutes or until golden brown. Cool for 10 minutes before carefully removing from pan to a wire rack.
5. Combine confectioners' sugar and orange juice; drizzle over warm coffee cake. Garnish with sliced almonds.

Orange Breakfast Rolls

Makes 6 servings
Cook Time: 20 Min

Ingredients

6 frozen bread dough rolls, thawed
4 teaspoons butter or margarine, softened
2 tablespoons sugar
1 teaspoon orange juice
1/2 teaspoon grated orange peel
1/2 cup confectioners' sugar
1 tablespoon orange juice
1/8 teaspoon grated orange peel

Directions

1. On a lightly floured surface, roll each piece of dough into an 8-in. rope. Flatten to 1-1/2-in. wide strip. Combine the butter, sugar, orange juice and peel; spread over dough. Roll up jelly-roll style, starting with a short side.
2. Pinch ends to seal. Place in a greased square baking dish. Cover and let stand in a warm place until doubled, about 45 minutes.
3. Bake on Hi for 18-22 minutes or until golden brown. Combine glaze ingredients and drizzle over warm rolls.

Pecan Breakfast Loaf

Makes 16 servings
Cook Time: 35 Min

Ingredients

2 (8 ounce) cans refrigerated crescent rolls
2 tablespoons butter or margarine, softened
1/2 cup sugar
1/4 cup chopped pecans
2 teaspoons ground cinnamon
1/4 cup pecan halves
1/4 cup confectioners' sugar
2 tablespoons butter or margarine
2 tablespoons honey
1 teaspoon vanilla extract

Directions

1. Separate crescent dough into 16 triangles. Spread each with butter. Combine sugar, chopped pecans and cinnamon; sprinkle over triangles.
2. Beginning at the wide end, roll up each triangle. In a greased loaf pan, place rolls, point side down, widthwise in two layers.
3. Bake on Hi for 35-40 minutes or until golden brown. Cool for 10 minutes before removing from pan to a wire rack.
4. Top with pecan halves. In a saucepan, combine glaze ingredients; bring to a boil, stirring constantly. Cool for 5 minutes. Drizzle over warm bread.

Pumpkin Muffins

Makes 12 servings

Ingredients

2 cups canned pumpkin
2 1/2 cups flour
1 3/4 cups sugar
3 eggs
1 1/3 cups oil
1/4 cup water
2 teaspoons vanilla
2 teaspoons cinnamon
2 teaspoons baking soda
1/2 teaspoon salt
3/4 cup mini chocolate chip

Directions

1. Combine all ingredients in mixing bowl. Mix until moistened.
2. Put in greased muffin tins. Bake on Hi until Golden Brown.

Raspberry Breakfast Braid
Makes 12 servings

Ingredients
2 cups packaged baking mix
1 (3 ounce) package cream cheese
1/4 cup butter or margarine
1/3 cup milk
1/2 cup Smucker's® Red Raspberry Preserves
1 cup powdered sugar
1/4 teaspoon almond extract
1/4 teaspoon vanilla
1 tablespoon milk, plus more if needed

Directions
1. In medium bowl, measure baking mix. Cut in cream cheese and butter until mixture is crumbly. Stir in milk. Turn dough onto a lightly floured surface and knead lightly 10 to 12 times.
2. Roll dough into a rectangle. Turn onto greased baking sheet. Spread preserves lengthwise down center 1/3 of dough. Make 2 1/2-inch cuts at 1-inch intervals on long sides. Fold strips over filling.
3. Bake on Hi for 12 to 15 minutes or until lightly browned. Combine all glaze ingredients, adding enough milk for desired drizzling consistency. Drizzle over coffee cake.

Sausage Breakfast Pizza
Makes 8 servings
Cook Time: 15 Min

Ingredients
1 (13.8 ounce) package refrigerated pizza crust dough
1 pound Bob Evans® Original Recipe Sausage Roll
8 ounces pre-sliced mushrooms
1 cup diced tomato
2 cups shredded pizza blend cheese
4 eggs

Directions
1. Unroll dough and press into a greased baking dish, covering bottom of pan and 2 inches up sides of dish.
2. Crumble and cook sausage and mushrooms in medium skillet until browned. Drain well on paper towels.

3. Spread sausage, mushrooms and tomatoes over crust. Top with shredded cheese. In small bowl, whisk eggs until well combined.
4. Pour over pizza. Bake on Hi for 13 to 15 minutes or until eggs are set and crust is brown.

Sausage Breakfast Wraps
Makes 10 servings
Cook Time: 30 Min

Ingredients
1 pound turkey Italian sausage links, casings removed
1 medium sweet red pepper, diced
1 small onion, diced
4 (8 ounce) cartons frozen egg substitute, thawed
1 (4 ounce) can chopped green chilies
1 teaspoon chili powder
10 (8 inch) flour tortillas, warmed
1 1/4 cups salsa

Directions
1. In a nonstick skillet, cook sausage over medium heat until no longer pink; drain. Transfer to a baking dish coated with nonstick cooking spray.
2. Sprinkle with red pepper and onion. Combine the egg substitute, green chilies and chili powder; pour over sausage mixture.
3. Bake on Hi uncovered for 30-35 minutes or until set. Break up sausage mixture with a spoon. Place 2/3 cup down the center of each tortilla; top with salsa. Fold one end over sausage mixture, then fold two sides over.

Sausage Cake
Makes 12 servings
Cook Time: 1 Hr 30 Min

Ingredients
1 cup raisins
3 cups boiling water
1 pound ground pork sausage
1 1/2 cups white sugar
1 1/2 cups brown sugar
2 eggs, lightly beaten
3 cups all-purpose flour
1 teaspoon ground ginger
1 teaspoon baking powder
1 teaspoon pumpkin pie spice
1 teaspoon baking soda
1 cup cold coffee
1 cup chopped walnuts

Directions
1. Place raisins in a bowl and cover with boiling water; set aside for 5 to 10 minutes. Drain well and dry raisins in cloth, set aside.
2. Place sausage in a large, deep skillet. Cook over medium-high heat until lightly brown. Drain, crumble into small pieces and set aside.
3. In a large bowl, combine sausage, white sugar and brown sugar; stir until mixture is well blended. Add eggs and beat well.
4. In a separate bowl, sift together flour, ginger, baking powder and pumpkin pie spice. Stir baking soda into coffee. Add flour mixture and coffee alternately to meat mixture, beating well after each addition.
5. Fold raisins and walnuts into cake batter. Turn batter into well-greased and floured Bundt cake pan.
6. Bake on Hi for 65 to 75 minutes or until done. Cool 15 minutes in pan before turning out onto serving platter.

Sausage Roll
Makes 12 servings
Cook Time: 30 Min

Ingredients
2 (1 pound) loaves frozen white bread dough
1 tablespoon vegetable oil
1 pound ground pork sausage
1 pound ground spicy pork sausage
1/2 large green bell pepper, chopped
1 (6 ounce) can canned mushrooms
2 cups shredded mozzarella cheese
1 egg
2 tablespoons water

Directions
1. Rub the frozen bread dough with vegetable oil, cover and allow to thaw overnight at room temperature.
2. Place sausage in a large, deep skillet. Cook over medium-high heat until evenly brown. Drain, crumble and set aside.
3. Roll out one loaf of bread and place on an ungreased sheet. Layer cooked sausage, green peppers, mushrooms, and cheese on top of bread.
4. Leave 1 inch border at the edges bare. Roll out second loaf of bread and place over bread and filling. Enclose filling by pinching edges of both loaves together.
5. In a small bowl, beat together egg and water. Brush surface of roll with egg wash. Bake on Hi for 25 to 30 minutes, or until golden brown.

Tasty Breakfast Burritos
Makes 8 servings
Cook Time: 10 Min

Ingredients
2 pounds ground pork sausage
12 eggs, beaten
1 (4 ounce) can chopped green chile peppers, drained
8 (10 inch) flour tortillas
8 ounces Cheddar cheese, shredded
1 teaspoon all-purpose flour
1 cup milk

Directions
1. Place sausage in a large, deep skillet. Cook over medium high heat until evenly brown. Drain, reserving 2 tablespoons drippings; set sausage aside.
2. Add the eggs and green chiles to the skillet; cook, stirring occasionally, until eggs are scrambled and set.
3. Lightly grease a baking pan. Place the tortillas on a counter top or other clean surface. Cover each tortillas with portions on sausage, cheese and eggs. Roll up the tortillas and place them seam side down in the baking dish.
4. Heat reserved sausage drippings in the skillet. Sprinkle on the flour and stir. Add milk, stirring constantly, until the gravy begins to thicken. Pour the gravy on top of the tortilla rolls.
5. Bake on Hi for 10 to 15 minutes, until gravy is bubbly.

Upside Down Cake
Makes 4 servings
Cook Time: 20 Min

Ingredients
2 tablespoons olive oil
3 large baking potatoes, peeled and diced
1/2 cup chopped red bell pepper
2 cloves garlic, chopped
1/2 cup chopped onion
salt and pepper to taste
10 slices bacon
4 eggs
1 teaspoon milk
1 cup shredded Cheddar cheese

Directions
1. Heat olive oil in a large skillet over medium heat. Add potatoes, red bell pepper, garlic and onion, and cook, stirring occasionally until potatoes are tender. Cover the pan with a lid for faster cooking.
2. Line the bottom of a cake pan with parchment paper. Set aside.
3. Fry bacon in a skillet over medium heat, or cook in the microwave, until crisp. Drain, crumble and set aside. Sprinkle the cheese in the bottom of the prepared pan.
4. Sprinkle bacon crumbles evenly over the cheese. Scoop the potato mixture into the pan so it is evenly distributed. Whisk together eggs and milk with a fork, and season with a little salt and pepper. Pour evenly over the food in the pan.
5. Bake on Hi for 20 minutes, just until the egg is set. Remove from the oven and run a knife around the outer edge. Flip onto a serving plate, and remove the parchment paper.

Dessert

Apple Crumb Pie
Makes 6 servings
Cook Time: 45 Min

Ingredients
Pastry for a single-crust 9-inch pie
6 cups chopped, peeled tart apples
2 tablespoons butter, melted
2 tablespoons sour cream
4 teaspoons lemon juice
1/2 cup sugar
1 tablespoon all-purpose flour
1/2 teaspoon ground cinnamon
1/2 teaspoon ground nutmeg
1/2 cup all-purpose flour
1/2 cup sugar
1/4 cup cold butter

Directions
1. Line a pie plate with pastry; flute edges. In a large bowl, combine the apples, butter, sour cream, lemon juice, sugar, flour, cinnamon and nutmeg. Spoon into pastry shell.
2. For topping, combine flour and sugar in a bowl; cut in butter until mixture resembles coarse crumbs. Sprinkle over filling.
3. Bake on Hi for 45-50 minutes or until the filling is bubbly and the apples are tender. Cool on a wire rack.

Apple Pie
Makes 8 servings
Cook Time: 40 Min

Ingredients
1/2 cup sugar
1/2 cup packed brown sugar
3 tablespoons all-purpose flour
1 teaspoon ground cinnamon
1/4 teaspoon ground ginger
1/4 teaspoon ground nutmeg
7 cups thinly sliced pared apples
1 tablespoon lemon juice
1 Pastry for double-crust pie (9 inches)
1 tablespoon butter or margarine
1 egg white
Additional sugar

Directions
1. In a small bowl, combine sugar, flour and spices; set aside. In a large bowl, toss apples with lemon juice. Add sugar mixture; toss well to coat. Line a pie pan with half the pastry.
2. Place apple filling into crust; dot with butter. Roll out remaining pastry to fit top of pie. Cut a few slits in top.
3. Beat egg white until foamy; brush over pastry. Sprinkle sugar on top. Bake on Hi for 40 minutes until golden.

Apple Pumpkin Desserts
Makes 8 servings
Cook Time: 25 Min

Ingredients
1 (21 ounce) can apple pie filling
1 (15 ounce) can pumpkin
1 (14 ounce) can EAGLE BRAND® Sweetened Condensed Milk
2 large eggs
1 teaspoon ground cinnamon
1/2 teaspoon ground nutmeg
1/2 teaspoon salt
1 cup gingersnap crumbs
2 tablespoons butter or margarine, melted

Directions
1. Spoon equal portions of apple filling into 8 lightly greased custard cups.
2. In large bowl, combine pumpkin, sweetened condensed milk, eggs, cinnamon, nutmeg and salt; mix well. Spoon equal portions over apple filling.
3. Combine gingersnap crumbs and butter in a small bowl. Sprinkle over pumpkin filling. Place cups on baking pan.
4. Bake on Hi for 10 minutes. Reduce temperature and bake 15 minutes longer or until set. Cool. Serve warm. Store leftovers covered in refrigerator.

Banana Rice Pudding
Makes 8 servings

Ingredients
1 cup white rice or 1 cup brown rice
2 1/2 cups water
3/4 cup sweetened condensed milk
3 tablespoons pure vanilla extract
3 tablespoons cinnamon
1 tablespoon nutmeg
1 -2 banana
1/2 cup brown sugar

Directions
1. Cook up rice using regular directions and then set aside.
2. Mix Rice, sweetened condensed milk, vanilla, cinnamon, brown sugar, nutmeg and banana. Mix well.
3. Check to see if this is to your liking, add more vanilla or cinnamon depending on what you like.
4. In large flan pan (fluted white round pan/glass - Looks like a flan pan) Or two square pans (cooked separately). Cook 30 minutes on HI or until set.

Blueberry Dessert Squares
Makes 9 servings
Cook Time: 45 Min

Ingredients
1 cup all-purpose flour
1 cup quick-cooking oats
1 cup packed brown sugar
1/2 teaspoon salt
1/2 cup shortening
2 1/2 cups fresh or frozen blueberries
1/4 cup sugar

Directions
1. In a large bowl, combine the flour, oats, brown sugar and salt. Cut in shortening until crumbly.
2. Press half of the mixture into a greased baking dish. Bake on Hi for 10 minutes or until brown around the edges.
3. Combine the blueberries and sugar; sprinkle over crust. Top with remaining oat mixture; press down gently.
4. Bake 35-40 minutes longer or until golden brown. Serve warm.

Blueberry Pie
Makes 8 servings
Cook Time: 40 Min

Ingredients
1 1/4 cups white sugar
3 tablespoons quick-cooking tapioca
1/2 teaspoon ground cinnamon
3 cups blueberries
1 tablespoon lemon juice
1 tablespoon butter
1 pastry for a 9 inch double crust pie

Directions
1. Roll out half the pastry and line a pie pan; trim crust to the rim of the pan. Loosely cover with plastic wrap and refrigerate.
2. Combine sugar, tapioca, and cinnamon. Toss sugar mixture with blueberries in a mixing bowl and sprinkle with lemon juice.
3. Let stand fifteen minutes. Meanwhile, roll out the top crust into a 10-inch circle. Cut into half-inch strips. Pour blueberry mixture into chilled pie shell and dot with butter.
4. Add the pastry strips one at a time, weaving a lattice. Flute edges. 3. Place pie on a baking sheet to catch drips. Bake on Hi for 40 to 50 minutes, until filling is bubbly and crust is light brown. Cool completely before serving.

Brownie Cookies
Makes 18 servings
Cook Time: 10 Min

Ingredients
2/3 cup shortening
1 1/2 cups packed brown sugar
1 tablespoon water
1 tablespoon vanilla extract
2 eggs
1 1/2 cups all-purpose flour
1/3 cup baking cocoa
1/2 teaspoon salt
1/4 teaspoon baking soda
2 cups semisweet chocolate chips
1/2 cup chopped walnuts or pecans

Directions
1. In a large mixing bowl, cream shortening, sugar, water and vanilla. Beat in eggs.
2. Combine flour, cocoa, salt and baking soda; gradually add to creamed mixture and beat just until blended.

3. Stir in chocolate chips and nuts if desired. Drop by rounded teaspoonfuls 2 in. apart on ungreased baking sheets.
4. Bake on Hi for 7-9 minutes; do not overbake. Cool 2 minutes before removing to wire racks. (These will have to be cook in multiple batches)

Brownie Cups
Makes 18 servings
Cook Time: 35 Min

Ingredients
1 cup butter or margarine
1 cup semisweet chocolate chips
1 cup chopped pecans
4 eggs
1 1/2 cups sugar
1 cup all-purpose flour
1 teaspoon vanilla extract

Directions
1. In a saucepan over low heat, melt the butter and chocolate chips, stirring until smooth. Cool. Add pecans; stir until well-coated. In a bowl, combine eggs, sugar, flour and vanilla.
2. Fold in chocolate mixture. Fill paper-lined muffin cups two-thirds full. Bake on hi for 35-38 minutes or until a toothpick inserted near the center comes out clean.

Brownie Truffle
Makes 12 servings

Ingredients
16 ounces brownie mix
2 eggs
1/2 cup butter

Directions
1. In bowl place mix, eggs & melted butter. Mix and put into 8 x 8 pan or use your nuwave round pan, grease pan.
2. Place mix in pan and bake for 30 minutes on Hi.
2 let cool 30 minutes.

Butter Crisps
Makes 24 servings

Ingredients
1 cup butter
0.5 (8 ounce) package cream cheese
1 cup white sugar
1 egg
1 teaspoon vanilla extract
2 1/2 cups all-purpose flour

1/2 teaspoon baking powder

Directions
1. Cream together the butter and cream cheese. Gradually add sugar and egg continue beating until blended.
2. Add flour and baking powder gradually to butter/cream cheese mix. Chill dough 1-2 hours.
3. Roll out on floured board and cut in desired shapes. Bake on hi 6 minutes or until light brown
4. Frost with desired frosting.

Butterscotch Pecan Dessert
Makes 16 servings
Cook Time: 20 Min

Ingredients
1/2 cup cold butter or margarine
1 cup all-purpose flour
3/4 cup chopped pecans, divided
1 (8 ounce) package cream cheese, softened
1 cup confectioners' sugar
1 (8 ounce) carton frozen whipped topping, thawed, divided
3 1/2 cups milk
2 (3.4 ounce) packages instant butterscotch or vanilla pudding mix

Directions
1. In a bowl, cut the butter into the flour until crumbly; stir in 1/2 cup pecans. Press into an ungreased baking pan. Bake on Hi for 20 minutes or until lightly browned. Cool.
2. In a mixing bowl, beat cream cheese and sugar until fluffy. Fold in 1 cup whipped topping; spread over crust.
3. Combine milk and pudding mix until smooth; pour over cream cheese layer. Refrigerate for 15-20 minutes or until set. Top with remaining whipped topping and pecans. Refrigerate for 1-2 hours.

Cherry Cheesecake
Makes 9 servings
Cook Time: 15 Min

Ingredients
1 1/4 cups graham cracker crumbs
2 tablespoons sugar
1/3 cup butter or margarine, melted
11 ounces cream cheese, softened
1/2 cup sugar
2 eggs
1 teaspoon vanilla extract
1 (21 ounce) can cherry pie filling

Directions

1. In small bowl, combine cracker crumbs and sugar; stir in butter. Press into a greased square baking dish; set aside.
2. In a mixing bowl, beat cream cheese and sugar until smooth. Beat in eggs and vanilla just until blended; pour over crust.
3. Bake on Hi for 15-20 minutes or until almost set. Cool for 1 hour on a wire rack. Refrigerate for 8 hours or overnight. Spoon pie filling over top.

Cherry Pie
Makes 6 servings
Cook Time: 55 Min

Ingredients
1 1/2 cups all-purpose flour
1/2 teaspoon salt
1/2 cup shortening
1/4 cup ice water
2 (16 ounce) cans tart cherries
1 cup sugar
3 tablespoons quick-cooking tapioca
1/4 teaspoon almond extract
1/4 teaspoon salt
red food coloring
1 tablespoon butter or margarine

Directions
1. In a bowl, combine flour and salt; cut in shortening until crumbly. Gradually add water.
2. Tossing with a fork until dough forms a ball. Divide dough in half. Roll out one half to fit a 9-in. pie plate for bottom crust.
3. Drain cherries, reserving 1/4 cup juice. Mix cherries, juice, sugar, tapioca, extract, salt and food coloring if desired; pour into the crust. Dot with butter . Top with a lattice crust. Bake on Hi for 55-60 minutes.

Chocolate Caramel Brownies
Makes 15 servings
Cook Time: 30 Min

Ingredients
14 ounces caramels
1/2 cup evaporated milk
1 (18.25 ounce) package German chocolate cake mix
1/3 cup evaporated milk
3/4 cup butter, melted
1/4 cup chopped pecans
2 cups milk chocolate chips

Directions

1. Peel caramels and place in a microwave-safe bowl. Stir in 1/2 cup evaporated milk. Heat and stir until all caramels are melted.
2. Grease a baking dish.
3. In a large mixing bowl, mix together cake mix, 1/3 cup evaporated milk, melted butter, and chopped pecans. Place 1/2 of the batter in prepared baking pan.
4. Bake on Hi for 8 minutes.
5. Place the remaining batter into the fridge. Remove brownies from oven and sprinkle chocolate chips on top. Drizzle caramel sauce over chocolate chips.
6. Remove brownie mix from refrigerator. Using a teaspoon, make small balls with the batter and smash flat. Very carefully, place on top of the caramel sauce until the top is completely covered.
7. Bake for an additional 20 minutes. Remove and let cool.

Chocolate Cheesecake
Makes 16 servings
Cook Time: 15 Min

Ingredients
1 (16.5 ounce) package Refrigerated Chocolate Chip Cookie Dough
2 (8 ounce) packages cream cheese, softened
1 cup granulated sugar
4 (1 ounce) packets Pre-Melted Unsweetened Chocolate Flavor
2 (8 ounce) containers frozen whipped topping, thawed
1/2 cup Semi-Sweet Chocolate Morsels, melted

Directions
1. Grease a 9-inch springform pan.
2. Slice dough into 16 pieces. Cover bottom of prepared pan with pieces. Allow to soften for 5 to 10 minutes. Using fingertips, pat dough gently to cover bottom.
3. Bake on Hi for 15 to 17 minutes or until light golden brown. Cool completely in pan on wire rack.
4. Combine cream cheese, sugar and choco bake in a large mixing bowl until well blended. Add whipped topping; stir until just blended. Spoon over cookie crust; smooth top.
5. Drizzle with melted chocolate. Cover; refrigerate for 3 to 4 hours or overnight. Remove sides of pan.

Chocolate Chip Cookies
Makes 60 servings

Ingredients
2 1/4 cups all-purpose flour
1 teaspoon baking soda
1 teaspoon salt
1 cup (2 sticks) butter, softened
3/4 cup granulated sugar
3/4 cup packed brown sugar
1 teaspoon vanilla extract
2 large eggs
2 cups (12-oz. pkg.) Semi-Sweet Chocolate Morsels

Directions
1. Combine flour, baking soda and salt in small bowl. Beat butter, granulated sugar, brown sugar and vanilla extract in large mixer bowl until creamy.
2. Add eggs, one at a time, beating well after each addition. Gradually beat in flour mixture. Stir in morsels and nuts.
3. Drop by rounded tablespoon onto ungreased baking sheets. Bake on Hi for 9 to 11 minutes or until golden brown.
4. Cool on baking sheets for 2 minutes; remove to wire racks to cool completely.

Chocolate Chip Shortbread Cookies
Makes 30 servings

Ingredients
1 1/2 cups all-purpose flour
1/3 cup unsweetened cocoa powder
1/2 teaspoon salt
2 cups semi-sweet chocolate chips, frozen 1 hour
3/4 cup unsalted butter, diced at room temperature
1 cup sugar
1 large egg yolk
2 teaspoons vanilla extract
3/4 teaspoon almond extract
1 cup walnuts, coarsely chopped

Directions
1 Whisk flour, cocoa, and salt in small bowl to blend. Coarsely chop 1 1/2 cups chocolate chips in processor. With machine running, add butter, then 1/2 cup sugar through feed tube.
2. Add egg yolk and both extracts and process to blend. Using on/off turns, mix in walnuts, scraping down sides of bowl occasionally.
3. Add flour mixture and process just until dough comes together, about 1 minute. Transfer dough to large bowl. Using hands, mix in remaining 1/2 cup chocolate chips.
4. Using 1 tablespoon dough for each, shape dough into 1 1/2 inch diameter balls. Press each dough ball to 1/2 inch thickness; dip 1 side into remaining 1/2 cup sugar to coat.
5. Arrange cookies, sugar side up, on Nuwave baking sheet. Cook on Hi and bake until cookies are set and almost firm to touch.

Chocolate Cookies
Makes 33 servings
Cook Time: 10 Min

Ingredients
1 cup butter or margarine, softened
1 1/2 cups sugar
2 eggs
2 teaspoons vanilla extract
2 cups all-purpose flour
2/3 cup baking cocoa
3/4 teaspoon baking soda
1/2 teaspoon salt
confectioners' sugar

Directions
1. In a mixing bowl, cream butter and sugar. Add eggs, one at a time, beating well after each addition.
2. Beat in vanilla. Combine the flour, cocoa, baking soda and salt; gradually add to creamed mixture.
3. Cover and refrigerate for 1 hour or until easy to handle. Roll into 1-in. balls. Place 2 in. apart on ungreased baking sheets.
4. Flatten with a fork if desired. Bake on Hi for 8-10 minutes or until the edges are firm. Remove to wire racks. Dust warm cookies with confectioners' sugar.

Chocolate Raspberry Cake
Makes 4 servings

Ingredients
12 ounces lava cake mix
2 eggs
3 tablespoons hot water

Directions
1. In mixing bowl combine, lava cake mix, 2 eggs & water. Mix together well.
2. In 4 cup cake tin (included) - pour 3/4 full. Place in Nuwave on rack (4 ins).
3. Cook on Hi heat for 20 minutes. Cool for 5 minutes and serve.

Christmas Cookies
Makes 24 servings

Ingredients
2 cups butter
1 cup brown sugar
1 cup light molasses
1 egg, beaten
4 cups flour
1/4 teaspoon salt
1 teaspoon baking soda
1 teaspoon cinnamon
1 teaspoon ground cloves
1/2 teaspoon nutmeg

Directions
1. Grease Baking pan. Cream butter and sugar. Blend in molasses and eggs.
2. Sift dry ingredients together and stir into molasses-egg mixture.
3. Roll out dough on lightly floured board and cut. 6 into shapes with cookie cutters.
4. Bake on Hi for 5 -6 minutes or until barely brown.

Dutch Apple Dessert
Makes 8 servings

Ingredients
5 medium all purpose apples, pared, cored and sliced
1 (14 ounce) can EAGLE BRAND® Sweetened Condensed Milk
1 teaspoon ground cinnamon
1/2 cup cold butter or margarine
1 1/2 cups biscuit baking mix, divided
1/2 cup firmly packed brown sugar
2 tablespoons cold butter or margarine
1/2 cup chopped nuts

Directions
1. In medium bowl, combine apples, sweetened condensed milk and cinnamon.
2. In large bowl, cut 1/2 cup butter into 1 cup biscuit mix until crumbly. Stir in apple mixture. Pour into greased 9-inch square baking pan.
3. In small bowl, combine remaining 1/2 cup biscuit mix and brown sugar; cut in remaining 2-tablespoon butter until crumbly. Add nuts. Sprinkle evenly over apple mixture.
4. Bake on Hi for 1 hour or until golden. Serve warm with ice cream if desired. Store leftovers covered in refrigerator.

Easy Peanut Butter Cookies
Makes 60 servings

Ingredients
1 (14 ounce) can Sweetened Condensed Milk
1 1/4 cups Creamy Peanut Butter
1 large egg
1 teaspoon vanilla extract
2 cups biscuit baking mix
Granulated Sugar

Directions
1. In large bowl, beat sweetened condensed milk, peanut butter, egg and vanilla until smooth. Add biscuit mix; mix well. Chill at least 1 hour.
2. Shape dough into 1-inch balls. Roll in sugar. Place 2 inches apart on ungreased baking sheets. Flatten with fork in criss-cross pattern.
3. Bake on Hi for 6 to 8 minutes or until lightly browned (do not overbake). Cool. Store tightly covered at room temperature.

Fudgy Brownie Dessert
Makes 15 servings
Cook Time: 20 Min

Ingredients
1/2 cup sugar
1/4 cup cornstarch
1/4 cup baking cocoa
1 (12 fluid ounce) can fat-free evaporated milk
1/2 cup egg substitute
1 1/4 cups baking cocoa
1 cup sugar
3/4 cup all-purpose flour
1 teaspoon baking powder
1 cup unsweetened applesauce
1 cup egg substitute
1/4 cup vegetable oil
2 teaspoons vanilla extract
1 (8 ounce) container frozen reduced-fat frozen whipped topping, thawed

Directions
1. In a saucepan, combine sugar, cornstarch and cocoa. Stir in the milk until smooth. Cook and stir over low heat just until boiling. Remove from the heat; stir a small amount into egg substitute. Return all to pan; cook for 1 minute or until thickened. Refrigerate.
2. Meanwhile, for crust, combine cocoa, sugar, flour and baking powder in a bowl. Combine applesauce, egg substitute, oil and vanilla; add to the dry ingredients and mix just until blended. Pour into a baking pan coated with nonstick cooking spray.
3. Bake Hi for 20 minutes or until a toothpick inserted near the center comes out clean. Cool on a wire rack. In a mixing bowl, beat the chilled chocolate mixture until light. Fold in whipped topping; carefully spread over crust. Refrigerate for 2 hours.

Fudgy Brownies
Makes 15 servings
Cook Time: 40 Min

Ingredients
1 cup all-purpose flour
1/4 cup unsweetened cocoa powder
1/2 teaspoon baking powder
1/2 teaspoon salt
1 1/2 cups white sugar
3/4 cup melted butter
1 1/2 teaspoons vanilla extract
3 eggs
1/2 cup chocolate syrup (such as Hershey's®)
1 cup semisweet chocolate chips

Directions
1. Grease a baking dish. Mix together the flour, cocoa powder, baking powder, and salt in a bowl; set aside.
2. Whisk the sugar, butter, and vanilla extract in a mixing bowl. Add the eggs and chocolate syrup; mix until evenly incorporated. Stir in the flour mixture and chocolate chips; stir until just moistened and pour into the prepared baking dish.
3. Bake on Hi until the top is dry and the edges have started to pull away from the sides of the pan, about 40 minutes. Cool completely before serving.

Ginger Cookies
Makes 15 servings
Cook Time: 10 Min

Ingredients
3/4 cup butter (no substitutes), softened
1 cup sugar
1 egg
1/4 cup molasses
2 1/4 cups all-purpose flour
2 teaspoons ground ginger
1 teaspoon baking soda
3/4 teaspoon cinnamon
1/2 teaspoon ground cloves
1/4 teaspoon salt
Additional sugar

Directions
1. In a mixing bowl, cream butter and sugar. Beat in egg and molasses. Combine the flour, ginger, baking soda, cinnamon, cloves and salt; gradually add to the creamed mixture.
2. Roll into 1-1/2-in. balls, then roll in sugar. Place 2 in. apart on ungreased baking sheets. Bake on Hi for 10-12 minutes or until puffy and lightly browned. Remove to wire racks to cool.

Oatmeal Chip Cookies
Makes 48 servings
Cook Time: 15 Min

Ingredients
1 cup butter, softened
1 cup sugar
1 cup packed brown sugar
2 eggs
1 teaspoon vanilla extract
2 cups all-purpose flour
1 teaspoon baking soda
1/2 teaspoon baking powder
1/2 teaspoon salt
2 cups old-fashioned oats
2 cups semisweet chocolate chips

Directions
1. In a large mixing bowl, cream the butter, sugar and brown sugar. Beat in eggs and vanilla. Combine the flour, baking soda, baking powder and salt; add to creamed mixture.
2. Stir in oats and chocolate chips.
3. Drop by rounded tablespoonfuls 2 in. apart onto ungreased baking sheets. Bake on Hi for 11-12 minutes. Cool on wire racks.

Peach Cobbler
Makes 8 servings

Ingredients
1 Box White Cake Mix
1 Twelve Ounce Can of 7-Up
1/2 Cup of Sugar
8 Peaches

Directions
1. Peel and quarter your peaches. Place them in the baking dish. Sprinkle your sugar on top of the peaches.
2. In a separate bowl mix the white cake mix and your can of 7-Up. The mixture will be lumpy. Pour the cake mixture on top of the peaches.
3. Place dish in Nuwave and cook on Hi for about 15-20 minutes but check occasionally to see if the cake is a golden brown. Serve Hot.

Peanut Butter Blossoms
Makes 48 servings
Cook Time: 10 Min

Ingredients
1/2 cup Butter Shortening
1/2 cup Creamy Peanut Butter
1/2 cup firmly packed brown sugar
1/2 cup sugar
1 large egg
2 tablespoons milk
1 teaspoon vanilla
1 3/4 cups All Purpose Flour
1 teaspoon baking soda
1/2 teaspoon salt
Sugar
48 foil-wrapped milk chocolate pieces, unwrapped

Directions
1. Cream together shortening, peanut butter, brown sugar and 1/2 cup sugar.
2. Add egg, milk and vanilla. Beat well.
3. Sire together flour, baking soda and salt. Add to creamed mixture. Beat on low speed until stiff dough forms.
4. Shape into 1-inch balls. Roll in sugar. Place 2 inches apart on ungreased cookie sheet.
5. Bake on Hi for 10 to 12 minutes or until golden brown.
6. Top each cookie immediately with an unwrapped chocolate piece, pressing down firmly so that cookie cracks around edge. Remove from cookie sheets to cool.

Peanut Butter Brownie Pizza
Makes 12 servings
Cook Time: 15 Min

Ingredients
1 (9 ounce) package brownie mix
1 (8 ounce) package cream cheese, softened
1/3 cup peanut butter
1/4 cup sugar
3 bananas, sliced into 1/4 inch slices
1/2 cup orange or lemon juice
1/4 cup chopped peanuts
2 (1 ounce) squares semisweet chocolate
2 teaspoons butter (no substitutes)

Directions
1. Prepare brownie batter according to package directions and spread into a greased 12-in. pizza pan. Bake on Hi for 15-20 minutes or until a toothpick inserted near the center comes out clean. Cool completely on a wire rack.
2. In a mixing bowl, beat the cream cheese, peanut butter and sugar until smooth. Spread over crust. Toss bananas with juice; drain well. Arrange bananas over cream cheese mixture. Sprinkle with peanuts.
3. In a microwave, melt chocolate and butter. Drizzle over bananas. Refrigerate until chocolate is set.

Peanut Butter Brownies
Makes 48 servings
Cook Time: 20 Min

Ingredients
1 1/2 cups butter or margarine, divided
3/4 cup baking cocoa, divided
4 eggs
2 cups sugar
1 teaspoon vanilla extract
1 1/2 cups all-purpose flour
1/2 teaspoon salt
1 (18 ounce) jar chunky peanut butter
1/3 cup milk
10 large marshmallows
2 cups confectioners' sugar

Directions
1. In a saucepan, melt 1 cup butter; stir in 1/2 cup cocoa until smooth. Remove from the heat. In a mixing bowl, combine the eggs, sugar and vanilla; beat for 1 minute. Combine flour and salt; gradually add to egg mixture. Beat in cocoa mixture; mix well. Transfer to a greased baking pan. Bake on Hi for 18-22 minutes or until toothpick inserted near the center comes out clean. Place on a wire rack.
2. Meanwhile, place peanut butter in a microwave-safe bowl. Microwave, uncovered, at 50% powder for 2 minutes, stirring once. Stir until peanut butter is blended. Spread peanut butter over warm brownies. Refrigerate for 45 minutes or until peanut butter is set.
3. Place the remaining cocoa in a heavy saucepan. Stir in the milk until smooth; add the marshmallows and remaining butter. Cook and stir over medium heat until butter and marshmallows are melted and mixture is smooth.
4. Remove form the heat. Gradually stir in confectioners' sugar. Spread over peanut butter layer. Refrigerate for at least 30 minutes. Cut into squares.

Peanut Butter Cookies
Makes 24 servings
Cook Time: 10 Min

Ingredients
3 tablespoons butter
2 tablespoons reduced fat peanut butter
1/2 cup packed brown sugar
1/4 cup sugar
1 egg white
1 teaspoon vanilla extract
1 cup all-purpose flour
1/4 teaspoon baking soda
1/8 teaspoon salt

Directions
1. In a large mixing bowl, cream the butter, peanut butter and sugars. Add egg white; beat until blended.
2. Beat in vanilla. Combine flour, baking soda and salt; gradually add to the creamed mixture. Shape into an 8-in. roll; wrap in plastic wrap. Freeze for 2 hours or until firm.
3. Unwrap and cut into slices, about 1/4 in. thick. Place 2 in. apart on baking sheets coated with nonstick cooking spray. flatten with a fork.
4. Bake on Hi for 6-8 minutes for chewy cookies or 8-10 minutes for crisp cookies. Cool for 1-2 minutes before removing to wire racks; cool completely.

Pumpkin Cheesecake
Makes 9 servings
Cook Time: 35 Min

Ingredients
3/4 cup finely chopped walnuts
3/4 cup graham cracker crumbs
1/4 cup sugar
1/4 teaspoon ground cinnamon
1/4 teaspoon ground ginger
1/8 teaspoon ground cloves
1/4 cup butter, melted
2 (8 ounce) packages cream cheese, softened
3/4 cup sugar
2 eggs, lightly beaten
1 cup canned pumpkin
1/2 teaspoon ground cinnamon, divided
2 tablespoons chopped walnuts

Directions
1. In a small bowl, combine the walnuts, cracker crumbs, sugar and spices; stir in butter. Press onto the bottom of an ungreased tart pan with a removable bottom.
2. For filling, in a large mixing bowl, beat cream cheese and sugar until smooth. Add eggs; beat on low speed just until combined.
3. Add pumpkin and 1/4 teaspoon cinnamon; beat on low speed just until combined. Pour into crust; sprinkle with walnuts and remaining cinnamon. Place pan on a baking sheet.
4. Bake on Hi for 35-40 minutes or until center is almost set. Cool on a wire rack for 1-1/2 hours. Store in the refrigerator.

Rhubarb Pudding
Makes 9 servings
Cook Time: 10 Min

Ingredients
1 cup graham cracker crumbs
2 tablespoons sugar
1/4 cup butter or margarine, melted
1 cup sugar
3 tablespoons cornstarch
4 cups chopped fresh or frozen rhubarb
1/2 cup water
3 drops red food coloring
1/2 cup whipping cream, whipped
1 1/2 cups miniature marshmallows
1 (3.4 ounce) package instant vanilla pudding mix

Directions
1. Combine the crumbs, sugar and butter; set aside 2 tablespoons. Press remaining crumbs into an ungreased baking dish. Bake on Hi for 8-10 minutes; cool.
2. For filling, combine sugar and cornstarch in a saucepan. Add rhubarb and water; bring to a boil. Cook and stir for 2 minutes or until thickened. Stir in food coloring if desired. Spread over the crust; chill.
3. Combine whipped cream and marshmallows; spread over rhubarb layer. Prepare pudding mix according to package directions for pie filling; spread over marshmallow layer.
4. Sprinkle with reserved crumbs. Cover and refrigerate for 4 hours or overnight.

Strawberry Pie
Makes 6 servings
Cook Time: 10 Min

Ingredients
1 (9 inch) unbaked pastry shell
3/4 cup sugar
2 tablespoons cornstarch
1 cup water
1 (3 ounce) package strawberry gelatin
4 cups sliced fresh strawberries
fresh mint

Directions
1. Line unpricked pastry shell with a double thickness of heavy-duty foil. Bake on Hi for 8 minutes. Remove foil; bake 5 minutes longer. Cool on a wire rack.
2. In a saucepan, combine the sugar, cornstarch and water until smooth. Bring to a boil; cook and stir for 2 minutes or until thickened.

3. Remove from the heat; stir in gelatin until dissolved. Refrigerate for 15-20 minutes or until slightly cooled.
4. Meanwhile, arrange strawberries in the crust. Pour gelatin mixture over berries. Refrigerate until set. Garnish with mint if desired.

Strawberry Rhubarb Pie
Makes 8 servings
Cook Time: 40 Min

Ingredients
1 recipe pastry for a 9 inch double crust pie
2 cups diced rhubarb
2 1/2 cups hulled strawberries
1 cup white sugar
1/4 cup all-purpose flour
3 tablespoons butter, diced
1/4 teaspoon ground nutmeg
1 tablespoon white sugar
1 teaspoon ground cinnamon

Directions
1. Divide the pie pastry in half; roll out half into a circle on a floured work surface, and line a 9-inch pie dish with bottom crust. Roll the remaining half out into a 10-inch circle on a floured work surface, and set aside.
2. Mix the rhubarb, whole strawberries, 1 cup of sugar, flour, butter, and nutmeg together in a bowl. Pour the filling into the crust-lined pie dish.
3. Cut the remaining crust into 3/4-inch wide strips (use a scalloped edge pastry cutter for a prettier crust). Moisten the rim of the filled bottom crust with a bit of water, and lay the two longest strips in a cross in the middle of the pie.
4. Working from the next longest down to the shortest strips, alternate horizontal and vertical strips, weaving the strips as you go.
5. Press the lattice strips down onto the bottom crust edge to seal, and trim the top crust strips neatly. Mix 1 tablespoon of sugar with cinnamon in a small bowl, and set aside.
6. Bake on Hi for 10 minutes; reduce heat level 2 or 3 levels Remove pie. Sprinkle the top with the cinnamon-sugar mixture, and return to nuwave oven; bake until the crust is golden brown and the filling is bubbling, about 30 more minutes.

Strawberry Shortcake
Makes 12 servings

Ingredients
3 cups fresh strawberries, washed and sliced
1/2 cup sugar
2 1/3 baking mix (Bisquick)
1/2 cup milk
3 tablespoons sugar
3 tablespoons butter or 3 tablespoons margarine

Directions
1.Mix strawberries with sugar, set aside. Stir in baking mix, milk, sugar, and butter until soft dough forms.
2. Form into small balls and place on bottom liner pan that has been sprayed with non-stick spray. Bake on power level high for 9 minutes.
3. Cut warm cake in half, fill with strawberries and top with your favorite whipped topping.

Strawberry/Rhubarb Crumb Pie
Makes 8 servings
Cook Time: 45 Min

Ingredients
1 egg
1 cup sugar
2 tablespoons all-purpose flour
1 teaspoon vanilla extract
3/4 pound fresh rhubarb, cut into 1/2 inch pieces
1 pint fresh strawberries, halved
1 (9 inch) unbaked pie shell
3/4 cup all-purpose flour
1/2 cup packed brown sugar
1/2 cup quick-cooking or rolled oats
1/2 cup cold butter

Directions
1. In a large mixing bowl, beat egg. Add the sugar, flour and vanilla; mix well. Gently fold in rhubarb and strawberries. Pour into pastry shell.
2. For topping, combine flour, brown sugar and oats in a small bowl; cut in butter until crumbly. Sprinkle over fruit. Bake on Hi for 10 minutes.
3. Reduce heat level and bake for 35 minutes or until golden brown and bubbly. Cool on a wire rack.

Streusel Rhubarb
Makes 12 servings
Cook Time: 1 Hr

Ingredients
1 cup all-purpose flour
1/3 cup confectioners' sugar
1/3 cup cold butter
1 1/4 cups sugar
1/4 cup all-purpose flour
1/2 teaspoon salt
2 eggs, lightly beaten
3 cups chopped fresh or frozen rhubarb
3/4 cup all-purpose flour
1/2 cup sugar
1/4 teaspoon ground cinnamon
1/3 cup cold butter

Directions
1. In a bowl, combine flour and confectioners' sugar. Cut in butter until crumbly. Press into a greased 9-in. square baking dish. Bake on Hi for 15-18 minutes or until brown around the edges.
2. Meanwhile, in a large bowl, combine the sugar, flour and salt. Add eggs; mix well. Fold in the rhubarb.
3. Pour over crust. For topping, combine the flour, sugar and cinnamon in a small bowl; cut in butter until crumbly. Sprinkle over filling.
4. Bake on Hi for 45-50 minutes or until rhubarb is bubbly. Cool on a wire rack.

Sugar Cookies
Makes 24 servings

Ingredients
1 (12 ounce) package sugar cookie dough
1 (12 ounce) package cookie dough (Pillsbury)

Directions
1. Cut sugar cookies in to approximately 24 cookies. In Nuwave oven place on baking sheet (or pan).
2. Cook for 4 – 6 minutes on hi until just starting to brown. Stop cooking once they start to barely show color.
3. As they will keep cooking even when you open up your oven. 2 Let cookies cook on pan/sheet for 4 - 5 minutes.

Walnut Apple Dessert
Makes 12 servings
Cook Time: 45 Min

Ingredients
8 cups sliced peeled tart apples
2 1/4 cups packed brown sugar, divided
2 teaspoons ground cinnamon
1 cup butter or margarine, softened
2 eggs
2 cups all-purpose flour
1 cup finely chopped walnuts, divided
Vanilla ice cream (optional)

Directions
1. Place apples in a greased baking dish. Sprinkle with 1/4 cup brown sugar and cinnamon. In a mixing bowl, cream butter and remaining brown sugar.
2. Add eggs. Stir in flour and 1/2 cup walnuts. Spread over apples. Sprinkle with remaining walnuts.
3. Bake on Hi for 45-55 minutes or until the apples are tender. Serve warm with ice cream if desired.

Pork

Asian Pork Chops
Makes 4 servings

Ingredients
1/3 cup black bean garlic sauce
3 large garlic cloves, minced
1 1/2 tablespoons soy sauce
1 1/2 tablespoons oriental sesame oil
1 tablespoon fresh lime juice
1 tablespoon finely chopped peeled fresh ginger
4 boneless center cut pork chops (about 8 ounces each)
4 baby bok choy, halved lengthwise
2 tablespoons chopped fresh cilantro
4 lime wedges

Directions
1. Whisk together black bean sauce, garlic, soy sauce, sesame oil, lime juice, and ginger in shallow dish.
2. Set 2 tablespoons marinade aside. Add pork to remaining marinade; let stand 20 minutes.
3. Remove pork from marinade; brush cut side of bok choy with reserved 2 tablespoons marinade.
4. Place pork on 4" rack and cook on HI for about 8~10 minutes per side. Grill bok choy until softened, about 8~10 minutes total.

Autumn Pork Tenderloin
Makes 2 servings
Cook Time: 40 Min

Ingredients
1/2 teaspoon salt
1/4 teaspoon pepper
1 (3/4 pound) pork tenderloin
1/2 cup apple juice
1 cup apple pie filling
1/4 cup raisins
1/4 cup chopped pecans
1/4 teaspoon ground cinnamon

Directions
1. Rub salt and pepper over pork. Place in a large resealable plastic bag; add apple juice. Seal bag and turn to coat. Refrigerate for 30 minutes.
2. Drain and discard apple juice. Place pork on a rack in a roasting pan. Combine the pie filling, raisins, pecans and cinnamon; spoon over pork.
3. Bake, uncovered, on Hi for 40-45 minutes or until a meat thermometer reads 160 degrees F Let stand for 5 minutes before slicing.

Bacon Wrapped Pork Medallions
Makes 4 servings
Cook Time: 30 Min

Ingredients
8 slices bacon
1 tablespoon garlic powder
1 teaspoon seasoned salt
1 teaspoon dried basil
1 teaspoon dried oregano
2 pounds pork tenderloin
2 tablespoons butter
2 tablespoons olive oil

Directions
1. Place the bacon in a large, oven-safe skillet, and cook over medium-high heat, turning occasionally, until lightly browned and still flexible, 6 to 7 minutes.
2. Drain the bacon slices on a paper towel-lined plate. Remove any excess bacon grease from the skillet. Combine garlic powder, seasoning salt, basil, and oregano in a small bowl. Set aside.
3. Wrap the pork tenderloin with the bacon strips securing with 1 or 2 toothpicks per strip of bacon. Slice the tenderloin between each bacon strip to create the medallions.
4. Dip both sides of the medallions in seasoning mix. Melt butter and oil together in the same skillet over medium-high heat.
5. Cook each medallion for 4 minutes on each side then transfer to baking dish.
6. Place dish into the nuwave and bake on Hi until the pork is no longer pink in the center, 17 to 20 minutes. An instant-read thermometer inserted into the center should read 145 degrees F (63 degrees C).

Baked Pork Chops

Makes 6 servings
Cook Time: 1 Hr 30 Min

Ingredients

6 pork chops
1 teaspoon garlic powder
1 teaspoon seasoning salt
2 egg, beaten
1/4 cup all-purpose flour
2 cups Italian-style seasoned bread crumbs
4 tablespoons olive oil
1 (10.75 ounce) can condensed cream of mushroom soup
1/2 cup milk
1/3 cup white wine

Directions

1. Rinse pork chops, pat dry, and season with garlic powder and seasoning salt to taste.
2. Place the beaten eggs in a small bowl. Dredge the pork chops lightly in flour, dip in the egg, and coat liberally with bread crumbs.
3. Heat the oil in a medium skillet over medium-high heat. Fry the pork chops 5 minutes per side, or until the breading appears well browned. Transfer the chops to a baking dish, and cover with foil.
4. Bake on Hi for 1 hour. While baking, combine the cream of mushroom soup, milk and white wine in a medium bowl.
5. After the pork chops have baked for an hour, cover them with the soup mixture. Replace foil, and bake for another 30 minutes.

Balsamic Roasted Pork Loin

Makes 8 servings
Cook Time: 1 Hr

Ingredients

2 tablespoons steak seasoning rub
1/2 cup balsamic vinegar
1/2 cup olive oil
2 pounds boneless pork loin roast

Directions

1. Dissolve steak seasoning in balsamic vinegar, then stir in olive oil. Place pork into a resealable plastic bag and pour marinade overtop. Squeeze out air and seal bag; marinate 2 hours to overnight.
2. Place pork into a glass baking dish along with marinade.
3. Bake on Hi basting occasionally until the pork reaches an internal temperature of 145 degrees F (65 degrees C), about 1 hour. Let the roast rest for 10 minutes before slicing and serving.

Barbeque Ribs

Makes 4 servings

Ingredients

4 lbs pork spareribs
1 cup brown sugar
1/4 cup ketchup
1/4 cup soy sauce
1/4 cup Worcestershire sauce
1/4 cup rum
1/2 cup chili sauce
2 garlic cloves, crushed
1 teaspoon dry mustard
1 dash ground black pepper

Directions

1. Cut spareribs into serving size portions, place it on 1" rack, and bake on HI for 6 minute per side.
2. In a bowl, mix together brown sugar, ketchup, soy sauce, Worcestershire sauce, rum, chili sauce, garlic, mustard, and pepper.
3. Coat ribs with sauce and marinate at room temperature for 1 hour, or refrigerate overnight.
4. Place ribs on 4" rack, and cook for 5~6 minutes per side.

BBQ Pork Pizza

Makes 4 servings
Cook Time: 18 Min

Ingredients

1 (13.8 ounce) package refrigerated pizza dough
1 (18 ounce) container barbequed pulled pork
1/4 red onion, thinly sliced
1/2 cup dill pickle slices
2 cups shredded mozzarella cheese

Directions

1. Grease a baking pan.
2. Roll the dough out into the prepared pan. Top the dough with the barbecued pork. Sprinkle with the red onions, and layer on the dill pickle slices.
3. Sprinkle mozzarella cheese evenly over the top. Bake on Hi until crust is golden and cheese is melted, about 18 minutes.

Berry Barbecued Pork Roast

Makes 12 servings
Cook Time: 1 Hr

Ingredients

1 (3 pound) boneless pork loin roast
1/4 teaspoon salt
1/4 teaspoon pepper
4 cups fresh or frozen cranberries
1 cup sugar
1/2 cup orange juice
1/2 cup barbecue sauce

Directions

1. Sprinkle roast with salt and pepper. Place with fat side up on a rack in a shallow roasting pan. Bake, uncovered, on Hi for 45 minutes.
2. Meanwhile, in a saucepan, combine the cranberries, sugar, orange juice and barbecue sauce. Bring to a boil. Reduce heat to medium-low; cook and stir for 10-12 minutes or until cranberries pop and sauce is thickened.
3. Brush some of the sauce over roast. Bake 15-20 minutes longer or until a meat thermometer reads 160 degrees F, brushing often with sauce. Let stand for 10 minutes before slicing. Serve with remaining sauce.

Caramelized-Onion Pork

Makes 4 servings
Cook Time: 40 Min

Ingredients

1 large sweet onion, thinly sliced
1 teaspoon sugar
2 teaspoons olive oil
1 (1 pound) pork tenderloin
1/4 teaspoon salt
1/8 teaspoon pepper

Directions

1. In a large skillet, cook onion and sugar in oil over medium-low heat until onion is tender and golden brown, about 30 minutes, stirring occasionally.
2. Place the pork in a baking dish coated with nonstick cooking spray. Sprinkle with salt and pepper. Top with onion mixture.
3. Bake, uncovered, on Hi for 40-45 minutes or until a meat thermometer reads 160 degrees F. Let stand for 5 minutes before slicing.

Chinese Pork BBQ Buns

Makes 16 servings

Ingredients

2 tablespoons vegetable oil
1 small onion, chopped
1 clove garlic, chopped
1/4 cup Kikkoman Oyster Sauce
2 tablespoons Kikkoman Less Sodium Soy Sauce
1 tablespoon sherry
1 tablespoon cornstarch
2 teaspoons sugar
1 pound Chinese barbecued pork, chopped
2 (11 ounce) packages refrigerated bread dough

Directions

1. In a wok or large skillet, heat oil over medium heat. Add onion and garlic; stir-fry until onion is soft. Remove from heat; add oyster sauce, soy sauce, sherry, cornstarch and sugar, stirring well to combine. Add pork and mix well.
2. Divide bread dough into 16 pieces and form each piece into a 2-inch ball. Flatten balls into 3-inch rounds. Place about 2 tablespoons pork filling in the center of each round.
3. Gather dough up and around filling by pleating along the edges. Place buns, sealed side down, on a nonstick baking sheet. Bake on Hi for 25-30 minutes or until buns are browned.

Garlic Pork Roast

Makes 6 servings
Cook Time: 2 Hrs

Ingredients

1 (5 pound) pork loin roast, backbone loosened
1/2 green bell pepper, finely chopped
1/2 cup thinly sliced green onions
1/2 cup chopped celery
8 cloves garlic, minced
1 teaspoon salt
1/4 teaspoon cayenne pepper

Directions

1. With a sharp knife, cut a deep pocket between each rib on meaty side of roast. Combine green pepper, green onions, celery and garlic; stuff deeply into pockets.
2. Season roast with salt and cayenne pepper. Insert meat thermometer. Place roast, rib side down, in a shallow roasting pan.
3. Bake, uncovered, on Hi for 2-3 hours or until thermometer reads 170 degrees F. Let stand for 15 minutes before carving.

Glazed Pork Tenderloin
Makes 4 servings
Cook Time: 25 Min

Ingredients
1/4 teaspoon salt
1/4 teaspoon pepper
1 (1 pound) pork tenderloin
2 sprigs fresh rosemary
1/2 cup pineapple preserves
1 tablespoon prepared horseradish

Directions
1. Combine salt and pepper; rub over pork. Place in baking pan coated with nonstick cooking spray. Place one sprig of rosemary under the pork and one on top. Bake, uncovered, on Hi for 10 minutes.
2. Meanwhile, in a saucepan, heat preserves and horseradish until preserves are melted; stir until blended. Remove top rosemary sprig.
3. Brush pork with 1/4 cup pineapple sauce. Bake 10-20 minutes longer or until meat thermometer reads 160 degrees F. Let stand for 5 minutes before slicing. Serve with the remaining sauce.

Herb Roasted Pork
Makes 8 servings
Cook Time: 3 Hrs

Ingredients
1 teaspoon rubbed sage
1/2 teaspoon salt
1/4 teaspoon pepper
1 clove garlic, crushed
1 (5 pound) boneless pork loin
1/2 cup sugar
1 tablespoon cornstarch
1/4 cup vinegar
1/4 cup water
2 tablespoons soy sauce

Directions
1. In a bowl, combine sage, salt, pepper, and garlic. Rub thoroughly all over pork.
2. Place pork in an uncovered roasting pan.
3. Bake on Hi for approximately 3 hours, or until the internal temperature reaches at least 145 degrees F (63 degrees C), depending upon your desired doneness.
4. Meanwhile, place sugar, cornstarch, vinegar, water, and soy sauce in a small saucepan. Heat, stirring occasionally, until mixture begins to bubble and thicken slightly.

5. Brush roast with glaze 3 or 4 times during the last 1/2 hour of cooking. Pour remaining glaze over roast, and serve.

Herbed Pork and Apples
Makes 14 servings
Cook Time: 2 Hrs 30 Min

Ingredients
1 teaspoon dried sage
1 teaspoon dried thyme
1 teaspoon dried rosemary
1 teaspoon dried marjoram
salt and pepper to taste
6 pounds pork loin roast
4 tart apples - peeled, cored, cut into 1 inch chunks
1 red onion, chopped
3 tablespoons brown sugar
1 cup apple juice
2/3 cup real maple syrup

Directions
1. In a small bowl, combine the sage, thyme, rosemary, marjoram, salt and pepper. Rub over roast. Cover, and refrigerate roast for 6 to 8 hours, or overnight.
2. Place roast in a shallow roasting pan, and bake on Hi for 1 to 1 1/2 hours.
3. Drain fat.
4. In a medium bowl, mix apples and onion with brown sugar. Spoon around roast, and continue to cook for 1 hour more, or until the internal temperature of the roast is 160 degrees F (70 degrees C). Transfer the roast, apples and onion to a serving platter, and keep warm.
5. To make the gravy, skim excess fat from meat juices. Pour drippings into a medium heavy skillet. Stir in apple juice and syrup.
6. Cook and stir over medium-high heat until liquid has been reduced by half, about 1 cup. Slice the roast, and serve with gravy.

Kalua Pork
Cook Time: 5 Hrs

Ingredients
5 pounds pork butt roast
1 tablespoon liquid smoke flavoring
2 1/2 tablespoons Hawaiian sea salt, divided

Directions
1. Rub liquid smoke and 1 1/2 tablespoons of the salt into the skin of the pork. Wrap well in foil, and seal completely. Place in a roasting pan.
2. Bake on Hi until an internal temperature of 160 degrees F (70 degrees C) is reached, about 4-5 hours.
3. Remove from oven and let cool before shredding. Sprinkle the shredded meat with the remaining 1 tablespoon of salt.

Plum Glazed Pork Ribs
Makes 6 servings
Cook Time: 1 Hr

Ingredients
4 1/2 pounds baby back pork ribs
12 fluid ounces chili sauce
10 ounces plum sauce
1/4 cup soy sauce

Directions
1. Prepare a shallow roasting pan with foil and spray the foil with non stick cooking spray.
2. Place ribs on foil and bake uncovered on Hi for 45 minutes.
3. While ribs are baking, heat chili sauce, plum sauce and soy sauce in a 1 quart saucepan to boiling; stirring constantly. Set aside.
4. After ribs have cooked for 45 minutes brush them with 1/2 cup of the sauce and place back in oven and bake until tender; 45 to 60 minutes.
5. While ribs are baking, brush them 2 or 3 times with the remaining sauce.

Porcini Pork Tenderloin
Makes 6 servings
Cook Time: 25 Min

Ingredients
1/2 cup extra virgin olive oil
1/2 cup herbes de Provence
4 cloves garlic, minced
3 pounds pork tenderloin
1/2 cup dried porcini mushrooms
1 cup boiling water
1/2 cup cognac
1 lemon, juiced
3 shallot, thinly sliced
1/2 cup heavy cream
1/4 cup unsalted butter, chilled and cut into small cubes
2 tablespoons honey
coarse salt and ground black pepper to taste

Directions
1. In a large measuring cup, mix together olive oil, herbes de Provence, and garlic. Place tenderloin in a large, rectangular baking pan. Pour olive oil mixture over meat, and turn to coat. Cover, and refrigerate for 3 hours.
2. Soak mushrooms in boiling hot water for 10 minutes to rehydrate.
3. Heat a large skillet over high heat. Remove meat from marinade, and discard any remaining marinade. Place meat in hot pan, and brown evenly. Return meat to baking dish.
4. Cook tenderloin on Hi for 15 to 20 minutes, or until the internal temperature of the meat is 150 degrees F (65 degrees C). Remove from oven, and allow it to rest for 5 minutes before slicing.
5. Meanwhile, combine the water in which the mushrooms were soaked, cognac, lemon juice, and shallots in a saucepan.
6. Cook over medium heat until liquid is almost gone. Pour in the cream. Bring to a boil, and then reduce heat to medium-low.
7. Chop mushrooms, and stir into the sauce. Continue cooking until the sauce thickens. Stir in the butter and honey. Season to taste with salt and pepper. Serve over sliced tenderloin.

Pork and Corn Stuffing Bake
Makes 4 servings
Cook Time: 30 Min

Ingredients
1 1/2 cups Cornbread Stuffing or Herb Seasoned Stuffing
1 (10.75 ounce) can Condensed Cream of Celery Soup or Condensed 98% Fat Free Cream of Celery Soup
1/2 cup whole kernel corn
1 small onion, finely chopped
1/4 cup finely chopped celery
4 boneless pork chops, 3/4-inch thick
1 tablespoon packed brown sugar
1 teaspoon spicy brown mustard

Directions
1. Stir the stuffing, soup, corn, onion and celery in a medium bowl. Spoon the stuffing mixture into a greased pie plate. Top with the pork.
2. Stir the brown sugar and mustard in a small bowl until the mixture is smooth. Spread the mixture on the pork.
3. Bake on Hi for 30 minutes or until the pork is cooked through.

Pork BBQ
Makes 10 servings
Cook Time: 4 Hrs

Ingredients
1 pound cubed beef stew meat
1 pound cubed pork loin
1 (10.75 ounce) can condensed tomato soup
1/4 cup Worcestershire sauce
1/2 cup vinegar
1 onion, diced
1 cup water

Directions
1. Combine together in a baking dish: beef cubes, pork cubes, tomato soup, Worcestershire sauce, vinegar, onion and water.
2. Bake on Hi for 4 hours. Add more water if liquid evaporates. When done, remove from oven and shred with a wooden fork or a potato masher.

Pork Hash Brown Bake
Makes 6 servings
Cook Time: 30 Min

Ingredients
1/4 cup all-purpose flour
2 teaspoons chicken bouillon granules
1/2 teaspoon salt
1 cup water
1/2 cup milk
1/4 cup sour cream
3 cups frozen O'Brien hash brown potatoes, thawed
2 cups cubed cooked pork
1 (10 ounce) package frozen mixed vegetables, thawed
1 (4 ounce) can mushroom stems and pieces, drained
1/2 cup crushed cornflakes
2 tablespoons butter or margarine, melted

Directions
1. In a saucepan, combine flour, bouillon, salt, water and milk until smooth. Bring to a boil; cook and stir for 2 minutes or until thickened. Remove from the heat; stir in sour cream.
2. In a large bowl, combine the potatoes, pork vegetables and mushrooms. Add the sour cream mixture; stir to coat well. transfer to a greased shallow baking dish.
3. Toss cornflakes and butter; sprinkle over the top. Bake, uncovered, on Hi for 30-35 minutes or until heated through.

Pork Pie
Makes 16 servings
Cook Time: 20 Min

Ingredients
3 pounds lean ground beef
2 pounds Italian sausage, casings removed
1 onion, chopped
4 potatoes - boiled and mashed
salt and pepper to taste
1/8 teaspoon ground cinnamon
1 pinch ground cloves
4 (9 inch) 9-inch pastry shell

Directions
1. In a large skillet over medium high heat, saute the ground beef and sausage for 10 minutes, or until browned.
2. Drain excess fat and transfer to a large bowl.
3. Combine the meat with the onion and mashed potatoes, mixing well. Season with salt and pepper, cinnamon and cloves to taste. Spoon mixture into two pie shells.
4. Cover each with the other pie shell. Remove foil pan from each top pie shell and, using a knife, poke some holes in each top pie shell to vent steam.
5. Bake on Hi for 15 to 20 minutes, or until pie crusts are golden brown.

Pork Roast with Tangy Sauce

Makes 10 servings
Cook Time: 1 Hr 40 Min

Ingredients
2 1/2 teaspoons chili powder, divided
1/2 teaspoon salt
1/2 teaspoon garlic salt
1 (4 pound) boneless rolled pork loin roast
1 cup apple jelly
1 cup ketchup
2 tablespoons white vinegar

Directions
1. In a bowl, combine 1/2 teaspoon chili powder, salt and garlic salt; rub over roast. Place roast fat side up on a rack in shallow roasting pan. bake, uncovered, on Hi for 1-1/2 hours.
2. In a saucepan, combine the jelly, ketchup, vinegar and remaining chili powder. Bring to a boil; cook and stir until the jelly is melted and mixture is smooth. Reduce heat; simmer, uncovered, for 2 minutes.
3. Brush 1/4 cup jelly mixture over roast. Bake 10-15 minutes longer or until a meat thermometer reads 160 degrees F.
4. Remove roast to a serving platter; let stand for 10-15 minutes. Skim fat from pan drippings. Stir in remaining jelly mixture; heat through. Slice roast and serve with sauce.

Pork Roast with Thyme

Makes 12 servings
Cook Time: 3 Hrs

Ingredients
5 pounds pork roast, trimmed
3 cloves garlic, sliced
1 teaspoon salt
1/2 tablespoon ground black pepper
3 bay leaves
1/2 cup cider vinegar
1 teaspoon dried thyme

Directions
1. With a small knife, pierce top of roast. Force garlic slices into the cuts. Sprinkle the roast with salt and pepper.
2. Place bay leaves in the bottom of the roasting pan, and set roast on top of bay leaves, fat side up. Mix vinegar and thyme in a small bowl, and pour over the top of the roast.
3. Bake on Hi for 3 hours, or until an internal temperature of 160 degrees F (70 degrees C) is reached. Using a baster or spoon, baste the drippings over the roast frequently while it is cooking. Let the roast rest for 10 minutes when done before slicing.

Pork Tenderloin alla Napoli

Makes 6 servings
Cook Time: 40 Min

Ingredients
1 tablespoon olive oil
2 (3/4 pound) pork tenderloins
2 Roma (plum) tomatoes, seeded and chopped
1/4 cup chopped green olives
1/4 cup dry white wine
1 teaspoon chopped fresh rosemary
2 cloves garlic, minced
1/2 teaspoon salt
1/4 teaspoon pepper
1/2 cup heavy cream

Directions
1. Heat the oil in a cast iron skillet over medium-high heat. Brown pork on all sides in the skillet.
2. Mix the tomatoes, olives, wine, rosemary and garlic in a bowl. Pour over the pork. Season with salt and pepper.
3. Place skillet with pork in the Nuwave and bake on Hi for 30 minutes, to a minimum internal temperature of 160 degrees F (72 degrees C).
4. Remove pork from skillet, leaving remaining tomato mixture and juices. Place skillet over medium heat, and gradually mix in the cream.
5. Stirring constantly, bring to a boil. Reduce heat to low, and continue cooking 5 minutes, until thickened. Slice pork, and drizzle with the cream sauce to serve.

Pork Tenderloin with Pineapple Salsa
Makes 6 servings
Cook Time: 35 Min

Ingredients
2 (1 pound) pork tenderloins
3 tablespoons brown sugar
3 tablespoons Dijon mustard
3/4 teaspoon minced fresh ginger root
2 cups chopped fresh pineapple
1/3 cup chopped sweet red pepper
1 small jalapeno pepper, seeded and chopped
2 green onions, chopped
1 tablespoon minced fresh cilantro
1 tablespoon brown sugar

Directions
1. Place pork on a greased rack in a foil-lined shallow roasting pan.
2. Combine the brown sugar, mustard and ginger; spread over pork.
3. Bake, uncovered, on Hi for 35-40 minutes or until a meat thermometer reads 160 degrees F. Let stand for 5-10 minutes before slicing.
4. In a bowl, combine the salsa ingredients. Serve with pork.

Red Wine Pork
Makes 8 servings
Cook Time: 2 Hrs

Ingredients
3 tablespoons bacon drippings
3 pounds pork roast
1/4 cup butter
2 cloves garlic, minced
2 carrots, diced
1 tablespoon chopped fresh parsley
1 bay leaf
1 teaspoon salt
1/8 teaspoon pepper
1 1/2 tablespoons tomato paste
1 1/2 tablespoons sugar
1 1/2 cups red wine
16 ounces fresh mushrooms, sliced

Directions
1. Heat bacon drippings in a large skillet over medium-high heat.
2. Brown roast on all sides. Remove roast to a casserole dish. Place butter, garlic, and carrots in the skillet. Reduce heat to medium. Stir in parsley, bay leaf, salt, pepper, tomato paste, and sugar. Pour in red wine, and stir to combine. Pour over pork roast.

3. Bake on Hi for 1 hour. Remove, and arrange mushrooms around the roast. Return to oven, and bake 1/2 hour.

Rhubarb Pork Chop Bake
Makes 4 servings
Cook Time: 40 Min

Ingredients
4 pork loin chops, cut about 3/4 inch thick
2 tablespoons vegetable oil
1 1/2 teaspoons minced fresh rosemary
1/4 teaspoon salt
1/8 teaspoon pepper
2 1/2 cups chopped fresh or frozen rhubarb (1/2-inch pieces)
4 slices day old bread, crusts removed and cubed
3/4 cup packed brown sugar
2 tablespoons all-purpose flour
1/2 teaspoon ground cinnamon
1/4 teaspoon ground allspice

Directions
1. In a large skillet, brown pork chops in oil. Sprinkle with rosemary, salt and pepper. In a bowl, combine the rhubarb, bread cubes, brown sugar, flour, cinnamon and allspice.
2. Place half of the rhubarb mixture in a greased baking dish. Top with chops and remaining rhubarb mixture. Cover and bake on Hi for 30-35 minutes. Uncover; bake 10 minutes longer or until juices run clear.

Roast Pork with Onion Stuffing
Makes 10 servings
Cook Time: 2 Hrs 30 Min

Ingredients
1 (3 pound) boneless pork loin roast
1 tablespoon olive or vegetable oil
2 teaspoons salt
1 teaspoon dried thyme
1/2 teaspoon pepper
4 large onions, chopped
1/4 cup butter or margarine
1/4 cup all-purpose flour
1 tablespoon lemon juice
1 teaspoon chicken bouillon granules
1 teaspoon salt
1/4 teaspoon ground nutmeg
1/4 teaspoon pepper
1 cup water

Directions
1. Rub roast with oil. Combine salt, thyme and pepper; sprinkle over roast. Place roast in a shallow baking pan.
2. Bake, uncovered, on Hi for 2 to 2-1/2 hours or until a meat thermometer reads 160 degrees F-170 degrees F. Meanwhile, in a skillet, saute onions in butter for 8-10 minutes or until tender. Stir in flour, lemon juice, bouillon, salt, nutmeg and pepper; add water.
3. Cook over medium heat for 2 minutes, stirring constantly. Cut roast almost all the way through into 3/8-in. slices. Spoon 1 tablespoon of stuffing between each slice.
4. Spoon remaining stuffing over roast. Bake, uncovered, on Hi for 30 minutes If desired, thicken pan juices to make gravy.

Roasted Pork Loin
Makes 12 servings
Cook Time: 2 Hrs

Ingredients
1/2 cup finely chopped onion
1/2 cup finely chopped celery
1/2 cup finely chopped green pepper
3 tablespoons butter or margarine
6 garlic cloves, minced
1 teaspoon salt
1 teaspoon pepper
1 teaspoon onion powder
1 teaspoon dried thyme
1 teaspoon paprika
1 teaspoon ground mustard
1/2 teaspoon garlic powder

1 (4 pound) boneless pork loin roast

Directions
1. In a skillet, combine the first 12 ingredients; saute until the vegetables are tender. Untie roast and separate.
2. Randomly cut 20 deep slits, 1 in. wide, on inside surface of roast. Fill slits with some of the vegetable mixture; retie roast. Place on a rack in a shallow baking pan.
3. Spread remaining vegetable mixture over the roast. Bake, uncovered, on Hi for 2-3 hours or until a meat thermometer reaches 160 degrees F-170 degrees F. Let stand for 10 minutes before slicing.

Roasted Pork Tenderloin
Makes 6 servings
Cook Time: 3 Hrs

Ingredients
2 pounds pork tenderloin
1/2 teaspoon ground sage
garlic salt to taste
1 (32 ounce) jar sauerkraut, drained
1/2 apple
1/2 onion
1/3 cup brown sugar

Directions
1. Rub tenderloin with sage and garlic salt. Place tenderloin in a baking pan or casserole.
2. Cover meat with half of the sauerkraut. Place the apple and onion, cut side down, on top of the sauerkraut. Cover with remaining sauerkraut. Sprinkle with brown sugar.
3. Cover and bake on Hi for 2 to 3 hours, until internal temperature has reached 160 degrees F (70 degrees C).

Savory Pork Roast I
Makes 9 servings
Cook Time: 1 Hr 20 Min

Ingredients
1 garlic clove, minced
2 teaspoons dried marjoram
1 teaspoon salt
1 teaspoon rubbed sage
1 (4 pound) boneless pork loin roast

Directions
1. Combine the seasonings; rub over roast. Place on a rack in a shallow roasting pan.
2. Bake, uncovered, on Hi for 1 hour and 20 minutes or until a meat thermometer reads 160 degrees F.
3. Let stand for 10-15 minutes before slicing.

Savory Pork Roast II
Makes 6 servings
Cook Time: 1 Hr

Ingredients
1 1/2 tablespoons fresh rosemary
2 teaspoons garlic salt
1/2 teaspoon dried thyme
1/4 teaspoon freshly ground black pepper
3 pounds boneless pork loin roast

Directions
1. In a large, resealable plastic bag, mix rosemary, garlic salt, thyme, and pepper.
2. Place pork roast in the bag, seal, and toss until thoroughly coated with the garlic salt mixture. Transfer to a medium baking dish.
3. Cook pork roast on Hi for 1 hour in the preheated oven, or to an internal temperature of 160 degrees F (70 degrees C).

Shepherd's Pie
Makes 4 servings

Ingredients
1 lb mild Italian sausage (3 links casings ermoved)
1 (2 lb) package of preparied mashed potatoes
1 medium green pepper, chopped
1 medium sweet onion, chopped
2 cups fresh corn, sliced off the cob
1 teaspoon kosher salt
3 medium garlic cloves, finley chopped
1 unbaked pie shell (9 inch)
2 tablespoons olive oil
1 cup shredded mozzarella cheese
pepper

Directions
1. In a medium skillet saute crumbled sausage untill lightly browned.
2. Add salt, green pepper, garlic and onion to sausage mixture and continue sauteing until soft.
3. Warm potato mixture to facilitate spreading.
4. Place sausage and pepper mixture into the pie shell.
5. Spread fresh corn over mixture.
6. Spread mashed potatoes to cover pie. Cover pie with mozzarella cheese.
7. Place pie on 1 inch rack and bake on power level 8 for thirty minutes.

South Shore Pork Roast
Makes 10 servings
Cook Time: 2 Hrs 20 Min

Ingredients
3 1/2 pounds boneless pork loin roast
1/4 cup butter or margarine
1 cup chopped onion
1 cup diced carrots
1 teaspoon paprika
3/4 cup chicken broth
2 tablespoons all-purpose flour
1/2 cup sour cream
1 tablespoon minced fresh parsley
1/2 teaspoon salt

Directions
1. In a large skillet over medium heat, brown roast in butter for 5 minutes on each side. Transfer to a roasting pan. In the same skillet, saute onion and carrots until crisp-tender.
2. Place around roast. Sprinkle with paprika. Add broth to pan. Cover and bake on Hi for 1-1/2 hours. Uncover; bake 50 minutes longer or until a meat thermometer reads 160 degrees F-170 degrees F.
3. Remove roast and vegetables to a serving platter; keep warm. Pour pan drippings to a measuring cup; skim fat.
4. Add water to measure 2-2/3 cups. In a saucepan, combine flour and sour cream until smooth. Add drippings, parsley and salt. Bring to a boil; cook and stir for 2 minutes or until thickened. Serve with the roast.

Stuffed Pork Chops
Makes 2 servings
Cook Time: 30 Min

Ingredients
2 tablespoons chopped celery
2 tablespoons chopped onion
2 tablespoons butter or margarine, divided
1/2 cup seasoned stuffing croutons
3 tablespoons milk
1 teaspoon minced fresh parsley
1/4 teaspoon paprika
1/8 teaspoon salt
1/8 teaspoon pepper
2 (1-inch thick) boneless pork loin chops
3/4 cup beef broth
1 tablespoon cornstarch
2 tablespoons cold water

Directions
1. In a skillet, saute celery and onion in 1 tablespoon butter until tender. Transfer to a bowl. Add croutons, milk, parsley, paprika, salt and pepper. Cut a pocket in each pork chop; fill with stuffing.
2. In a skillet, brown chops in remaining butter. Transfer to a greased square baking dish. pour broth into dish. Cover and bake on Hi for 30-35 minute or until a meat thermometer reads 160 degrees F. Remove chops and keep warm.
3. Pour the pan drippings into a saucepan; bring to a boil. Combine cornstarch and water until smooth; gradually stir into drippings. Cook and stir for 2 minutes or until thickened. Serve with the pork chops.

Tender Pork Spare Ribs
Makes 8 servings
Cook Time: 4 Hrs

Ingredients
1 cup brown sugar
1/2 cup fajita seasoning (such as Fiesta®)
2 tablespoons Hungarian sweet paprika
2 racks pork spareribs, fat trimmed
1 cup beer
3 cloves garlic, minced
1 tablespoon honey
3 tablespoons Worcestershire sauce
1 tablespoon prepared brown mustard

Directions
1. Mix the brown sugar, fajita seasoning, and paprika in a bowl. Rub both sides of the pork spareribs with the brown sugar mixture. Place the spareribs in a baking pan; cover and refrigerate overnight.
2. Whisk together the beer, garlic, honey, Worcestershire sauce, and mustard in a bowl. Set aside.
3. Tear off 2 large sheets of heavy duty aluminum foil and lay them shiny-side down. Place a rack of spareribs on each sheet, meaty-side up. Tear off 2 more sheets of foil and place them on top of the ribs, shiny-side up. Begin tightly folding the edges of the foil together to create a sealed packet. Just before sealing completely, divide the beer mixture evenly into each packet. Complete the seal.
4. Bake on Medium until the ribs are very tender, 3 hours and 30 minutes to 4 hours. Carefully open each packet, and drain the drippings into a saucepan. You may only need the drippings from one packet. Set ribs aside. Simmer the drippings over medium-high heat until the sauce begins to thicken, about 5 minutes. Brush the thickened sauce over the ribs.
5. Preheat your oven's broiler and set the oven rack about 6 inches from the heat source.
6. Place the ribs back into the oven and broil until the sauce is lightly caramelized, 5 to 7 minutes.

Tender Pork Tenderloin
Makes 4 servings
Cook Time: 1 Hr

Ingredients
1 (1 1/2 pound) fat-trimmed pork tenderloin
salt and pepper to taste
all-purpose flour for dusting
2 tablespoons vegetable oil
1 (8 ounce) bottle Russian-style salad dressing
3/4 cup honey
1 (1 ounce) envelope dry onion soup mix

Directions
1. Trim any excess fat from pork and pat dry with a paper towel. Season with salt and pepper.
2. Dust with flour, shaking off any excess.
3. In a large skillet, heat 1 to 2 tablespoons of vegetable oil over medium-high heat. Sear the pork in the oil, rotating to brown evenly all sides. Transfer to a baking dish just large enough to fit the tenderloin.
4. In a bowl, stir together the Russian-style salad dressing, honey, and onion soup mix. Pour evenly over the tenderloin, rolling the meat to coat on all sides. Cover with aluminum foil.
5. Bake, covered, on Hi for 30 minutes, basting with glaze every 10 minutes. Remove foil and continue

baking another 30 minutes, or until pork is no longer pink in the center.

Teriyaki Pork Tenderloin
Makes 6 servings
Cook Time: 25 Min

Ingredients
5 tablespoons low-sodium soy sauce
2 tablespoons olive oil
2 garlic cloves, minced
2 teaspoons brown sugar
1 teaspoon ground ginger
1 teaspoon coarsely ground pepper
2 (1 pound) pork tenderloins

Directions
1. In a large resealable plastic bag, combine the first six ingredients; add pork. Seal bag and turn to coat; refrigerate for 8 hours or overnight.
2. Drain and discard marinade. Place a tenderloin in a baking pan coated with nonstick cooking spray.
3. Bake, uncovered, on Hi for 25-35 minutes or until a meat thermometer reads 160 degrees F. Let stand for 5 minutes before slicing. Serve with pan drippings.

Tuscan Pork Roast
Makes 10 servings
Cook Time: 1 Hr 30 Min

Ingredients
3 garlic cloves, minced
2 tablespoons olive oil
1 tablespoon fennel seed, crushed
1 tablespoon dried rosemary, crushed
1 teaspoon salt
1/4 teaspoon pepper
1 (3 pound) boneless pork loin roast

Directions
1. In a small bowl, combine the first six ingredients; rub over pork roast. Cover and refrigerate overnight.
2. Place roast on a rack in a shallow roasting pan.
3. Bake, uncovered, on Hi for 1-1/2 hours or until a meat thermometer reads 160 degrees F, basting occasionally with pan juices. Let stand for 10 minutes before slicing.

Poultry

Asian Chicken Wings
Makes 10 servings
Cook Time: 55 Min

Ingredients
3 tbsp molasses
1/4 cup mirin
1/4 cup honey
2 tbsp soy sauce
2 tsp sesame oil
2 cloves garlic, minced
1 small shallot, minced
1 tsp freshly grated ginger
2 tbsp hoisin sauce (available in Asian markets)
1 tbsp black bean sauce
1 (10 oz) can beef consommé (not beef stock!)
1 tsp dried chili flakes, optional
3 lbs chicken wings, tips discarded, cut between joint into two pieces
3 green onions, minced
2 tbsp sesame seeds, optional

Directions
1. In a small bowl, combine marinade ingredients. Whisk thoroughly. This marinade can be made a day or two ahead and stored in the refrigerator.
2. In a shallow baking dish arrange wings, add sauce, cover and marinate 1 hour in refrigerator. With the Nuwave you may need to cook wings in batches.
3. Bake on Hi, uncovered, for 40 minutes until meat is tender. Remove from oven and transfer wings to an serving dish. Pour cooking juices into a saucepan and reduce over medium-high heat for 15 minutes.
4. Stir in white and light green parts of minced onions. Cook an additional 10 to 15 minutes, stirring regularly to keep it from burning, or until thick and sticky.
5. Pour half of sauce over wings and toss to coat thoroughly. Arrange on serving platter. Drizzle with a little of remaining sauce, sprinkle with remaining green onions and sesame seeds.

Baked Chicken and Stuffing
Makes 4 servings
Cook Time: 30 Min

Ingredients
4 chicken breasts (frozen)
11 ounces chicken soup (1 can)
1/2 cup butter, melted
1 pinch poultry seasoning
3 cups seasoned stuffing mix
1/4 cup water
4 slices swiss cheese

Directions
1. In a baking pan, place chicken & add slice of cheese to each breast. In seperate bowl combine chicken soup and 1/4 water.
2. Place soup mixture on top of chicken and cheese. Then crunch up stuffing into small bits, add to chicken.
3. The last step is to add the butter over the top (drizzle). This way the stuffing gets moist and crunchy. (cover with foil for the first 15-20 minutes.
4. Remove the last 10 - 15 minutes so top will cook. Bake on HI for 30-35 minutes.

Baked Chicken Legs
Makes 4 servings
Cook Time: 40 Min

Ingredients
4 chicken legs
1/2 cup extra virgin olive oil
1 tsp Worcestershire sauce
3 Tbsp Mediterranean spiced sea salt

Directions
1. Mix all the wet and dry ingredients in a bowl with lid, add the chicken legs and put the lid onto the bowl.
2. Shake/toss to coat the chicken legs completely. Put into fridge for 4-6 hours. Bake on Hi for 40 minutes.

Baked Chicken with Tomato Paste
Makes 4 servings
Cook Time: 45 Min

Ingredients
4-6 chicken thighs
1 can tomato paste
4 cloves of garlic, crushed
salt
juice of 1 lemon
2 large potatoes quartered
pepper
1/4 cup of olive oil
1 large onion sliced

Directions
1. In a mixing bowl, place olive oil, tomato paste, lemon juice, and garlic Add salt and pepper to taste In a baking dish, arrange chicken pieces and quartered potatoes.
2. Pour tomato paste over top and spread with a knife to even out and place sliced onions on top
3. Cover with foil and bake on Hi for approximately 45 minutes When chicken is almost done, remove foil and cook just enough to brown onions

Buffalo Chicken Dip
Makes 8 servings
Cook Time: 25 Min

Ingredients
1 - 8 oz. pkg cream cheese, softened
1 cup Frank.s Hot Pepper Sauce
1 cup blue cheese dressing
1 pkg. boneless skinless chicken breasts, cooked and cut into chunks
1 cup (4 oz.) shredded cheese (Cheddar or Mozzarella)
Crackers, chips or celery sticks

Directions
1. In a mixing bowl combine cream cheese, hot sauce and salad dressing. Stir in chicken. Spread into an ungreased baking dish. Sprinkle with cheese.
2. Bake on Hi uncovered for 22-25 minutes or until heated through. Served with crackers, chips or celery sticks.

Buffalo Chicken Pizza
Makes 8 servings
Cook Time: 20 Min

Ingredients
1 homemade or store bought pizza dough

3 boneless skinless chicken breasts, diced
1 small can tomato paste
1 cup water
hot sauce to taste 4 oz, or 1/2 cup
1 teaspoon smoked paprika
1 teaspoon cayenne pepper, optional
2 cloves garlic, grated
1/2 teaspoon oregano
olive oil
kosher salt
pepper
1/2 cup blue cheese
1 1/2 cups mozzarella cheese
1/3 green pepper, sliced
1/3 red pepper, sliced
1/4 medium onion, sliced
6-8, or a small bunch of green onions, chopped

Directions
1. Prepare chicken. Add salt, pepper, cayenne, and paprika to chicken. Preheat a large skillet. Drizzle with olive oil. Add chicken to skillet. Brown chicken.
2. Add tomato paste, water, hot sauce, and oregano. Bring to a boil, and reduce to a simmer. Simmer until sauce is very thick. Pre-bake pizza dough on Hi.
3. Add sauce and chicken to pizza dough. Then add 1 cup of the cheese. Then add the vegetables. Add blue cheese and the rest of the mozzarella cheese.
4. Bake on Hi until cheese has melted and edges are browned.

Chicken Alfredo Cupcakes
Makes 12 servings
Cook Time: 15 Min

Ingredients
Alfredo sauce (jar or homemade)
Canned chicken
Grated mozzarella cheese
Grated Parmesan cheese
Ricotta cheese
Wonton (egg roll) wrappers
Spray oil

Directions
1. Spray muffin tins with oil Cut wrappers into circles with cookie cutters(large and small) Line tin with one large wrapper, then layer about 1 teaspoon of chicken, each cheese, and sauce, a small wrapper and more filling, finishing with a small wrapper and topped with mozzarella and Parmesan cheese.
2. Bake on Hi for about 15 minutes until bubbly.

Chicken and Broccoli Casserole
Makes 6 servings
Cook Time: 45 Min

Ingredients
3 boneless, skinless chicken breasts
16 oz (one bag) frozen broccoli florets
2 tbsp butter
1 can cream of chicken soup
1 1/2 cups mayonnaise
1/2 tsp thyme
1/2 tsp savory
1/2 tsp rosemary
1/2 tsp curry powder
1/4 tsp sage
A pinch of salt
2 cups Monterrey Jack cheese, shredded.
Salt and pepper to taste

Directions
1. Grill or fry the chicken breasts until done, approximately 8 minutes on each side, medium-high heat or until no longer pink in the middle.
2. While the chicken is cooking, slightly under-cook the broccoli according to package directions. Add butter to the drained broccoli and salt to taste.
3. Layer the broccoli in the bottom of a casserole dish. Combine in a large mixing bowl the cream of chicken soup, mayonnaise, seasonings, and 1 cup of the shredded cheese.
4. Cut the chicken into 1/2 inch cubes and season with salt and pepper to taste. Fold the chicken pieces into the mayonnaise mixture.
5. Layer the chicken on top of the broccoli, and sprinkle the top with the remaining 1 cup shredded cheese. Sprinkle lightly with curry powder. Bake on Hi for 45 minutes.

Chicken and Jalapeno Quesadillas
Makes 2 servings
Cook Time: 5 Min

Ingredients
4 jalapeno-cilantro tortillas
2 tablespoons vegetable oil
1 1/2 cups mexican cheese (shredded)
1 1/2 cups roasted deli chicken (shredded)
1/4 cup fresh cilantro (chopped)

Directions
1. Brush 2 tortillas with oil. Place tortillas, oil side down, on baking sheet.
2. Sprinkle each with 1/4 of cheese, half of chicken, half of cilantro, and 1/4 of cheese, leaving 3/4-inch border.
3. Top each with 1 tortilla, pressing to adhere; brush top with oil. Bake quesadillas until filling is heated through and edges begin to crisp, about 2~3 minutes.
4. Using large metal spatula, turn each over and bake until bottom is crisp, about 1~2 minutes.
5. Transfer quesadillas to plates. Cut into wedges and serve.

Chicken Chilaquiles
Makes 4 servings
Cook Time: 20 Min

Ingredients
2 cups shredded skinless, boneless rotisserie chicken (from local grocery store or bake yourself if you have time)
1/2 cup chopped green onions
1/2 cup shredded Jack cheese with jalapeno (~2oz)
2 Tbsp grated Parmesan
1 tsp chili powder
1/4 tsp salt
1/4 tsp fresh ground black pepper
3/4 cup low fat milk
1/4 cup fresh cilantro, chopped
1 11oz can tomatillos, drained
1 4.5oz can chopped green chiles, drained
12 corn tortillas

Directions
1. Combine chicken, green onions, 1/4 cup Jack cheese (reserve other 1/4 cup), Parmesan, chili powder, salt, and pepper in a medium bowl. Place milk, cilantro, tomatillos, and green chiles in a food processor or blender.
2. Process till smooth. Pour 1/3 cup tomatillo mixture into the bottom of baking dish coated with cooking spray. Arrange 4 corn tortillas in dish and top with half of chicken mix.
3. Repeat layer with remaining tortillas and chicken mixture, ending with final layer of tortillas. Pour remaining 1 1/2 cups tomatillo mixture over tortillas and sprinkle with remaining Jack cheese. Bake on Hi for 20 minutes.

Chicken Cordon Bleu
Makes 6 servings
Cook Time: Cook Time: 15 Min

Ingredients
6 boneless skinless chicken breast halves, pounded to 1/2 inch thickness
6 pieces mozzarella string cheese
6 slices ham
1/2 cup butter, melted
1 cup seasoned dry bread crumb (Italian)
2 teaspoons granulated garlic
1/4 teaspoon salt
1/4 teaspoon pepper
toothpick

Directions
1. Lay out the pounded chicken breasts on a clean surface. Place a slice of ham on each piece, then one stick of cheese.
2. Roll the chicken up around the cheese and ham, and secure with toothpicks. Dip each roll in melted butter, then roll in bread crumbs.
3. Place on wire rack (lowest). Cook until outiside of chicken is is browned (crispy) and juices run clear. Cook until chicken starts to become golden brown.

Chicken Nachos
Makes 8 servings
Cook Time: 10 Min

Ingredients
3 boneless skinless chicken breasts
1 lb shredded cheese
1 can black beans
1 bag of tortilla chips or follow my chip recipe
1 10 oz sour cream
2 cups guacamole (see my recipe for organic guacamole)
2 fresh diced jalapenos
2 cups shredded lettuce
1 diced tomato
1/4 diced onion
2 cups salsa or (see recipe in my recipes)
1 large cookie sheet

Directions
1. Grill chicken with cumin, onions, peppers, and garlic. Place chips on baking sheet 1 layer cover with cheese and add second layer of chips.
2. Place more cheese spread even layer of black beans onto ships add more cheese place sliced chicken breasts spread evenly over pan of nachos.
3. Place in nuwave on Hi until melted about 5- 10 minutes dice onions, peppers, and shred lettuce

remove from oven garnish with lettuce, peppers, onions , jalapenos ,salsa sour cream and guacamole.

Chicken Nuggets
Makes 2 servings
Cook Time: 6 Min

Ingredients
1 egg
1 cup water
2/3 cup all-purpose flour
1/3 cup tempura mix (or 1/3 cup flour for a total of 1 cup if tempura mix is unavailable)
2 teaspoons salt
1 teaspoon onion powder
1/2 teaspoon Accent seasoning or 1/2 teaspoon tenderizing salt
1/4 teaspoon pepper
1/8 teaspoon garlic powder
4 chicken breast fillets, each cut into 6-7 bite sized pieces

Directions
1. Beat the egg and then combine it with 1 cup water in a small, shallow bowl and stir.
2. Combine the flour, salt, Accent, pepper, onion powder and garlic powder in a one gallon size zip lock bag.
3. Pound each of the breast filets with a mallet until about 1/4-inch thick. Trim each breast filet into bite sized pieces.
4. Coat each piece with the flour mixture by shaking in the zip lock bag. Remove and dredge each nugget in the egg mixture, coating well.
5. Then return each nugget to the flour/seasoning mixture. Shake to coat. Put nuggets, bag and all, in the freezer for at least an hour.
6. Cover and refrigerate remaining egg mixture. After freezing, repeat the "coating" process. Air fry the chicken Nuggets on Nu Wave Oven on 4" rack on HI for about 2 ~3 minutes per side (total 5 ~ 6 minutes) or until light brown and crispy.

Chicken Parmesan
Makes 4 servings
Cook Time: 10 Min

Ingredients
4 chicken, breasts-frozen
low-fat Italian salad dressing
seasoned bread crumbs
8 ounces 2% mozzarella cheese (shredded)
grated parmesan cheese
12 ounces pasta sauce

Directions
1. Dip chicken pieces in Italian dressing and roll in bread crumbs. Place on liner pan. Nu-Wave 8 minutes per side (or until done).
2. Open oven and spoon sauce on each piece and sprinkle with cheese. Cook 2 more minutes.

Chicken Skewers
Makes 4 servings
Cook Tim: 12 Min

Ingredients
1 1/2 cups fresh lime juice (12 limes)
3 garlic cloves, minced
2 teaspoons achiote paste
1 teaspoon dried oregano leaves
1 teaspoon ground cumin
1 1/2 lbs boneless skinless chicken thighs, cut into 1-inch pieces
2 jalapeno chiles
1 (20 ounce) jar guava shells in syrup
1 tablespoon cilantro, chopped fresh

Directions
1. Blend 1 cup lime juice, garlic, achiote paste, oregano, and cumin in processor until smooth.
2. Season marinade to taste with salt and pepper. Place marinade in medium bowl. Add chicken; stir to coat.
3. Cover and refrigerate chicken overnight. Place chilies on small baking sheet (on a 4" rack).
4. Roast until soft, about 10 minutes. Stem and seed chilies. Transfer chilies to processor. Add pureed guava, reserved guava syrup, cilantro, and remaining 1/2 cup lime juice.
5. Process until smooth. Season sauce to taste with salt and pepper. Transfer to medium bowl. (Sauce can be made 1 day ahead. Cover and refrigerate. 15 Bring to room temperature before using.).
6. Remove chicken from marinade. Divide chicken among 8 eight-inch wooden skewers.

7. Grill until chicken is cooked, turning once, about 6 minutes side. Serve, passing guava sauce separately.

Chicken Stroganoff
Makes 6 servings
Cook Time: 45 Min

Ingredients
1 Whole Cut-up Chicken or 6 pieces of whichever cut is preferred
1/2 Onion
4 oz Mushrooms
16 oz or 1 Pint Sour Cream
1/4 C White Wine

Directions
1. Fry Chicken pieces in pan skin side down in with oil only long enough to crisp and brown the skin.
2. Slice Onion and Mushrooms into strips and cook in pan with Chicken to soak up some of the flavor.
3. Place these ingredients into baking dish with Sour Cream covering them. Use White Wine to deglaze pan and add rendering to the casserole dish.
4. Bake on Hi for about 45 minutes to 1 hour or until meat falls off the bone. Remove skin from Chicken before serving. Salt and pepper to taste. Serve over noodles or rice.

Chicken with Orange Glaze
Makes 5 servings
Cook Time: 20 Min

Ingredients
1 - 7lb. oven stuffer chicken
¼ cup olive oil
1 tablespoon teriyaki sauce
2 tablespoons orange marmalade
Juice of ½ lemon
Dash of paprika
Dash of fresh ground black pepper
1 cup of fresh bread crumbs
1 head of Italian parsley . chopped
5 cloves of garlic . chopped
¼ cup of fresh grated Romano cheese
¼ cup of olive oil
Dashes of fresh ground black pepper
Dashes of sea salt

Directions
1. Combine all of the ingredients for the glaze.
Combine all of the ingredients for the stuffing.
2. Clean the chicken inside and out thoroughly and
then pat dry with paper towel. Clean all surfaces
thoroughly after doing this. Place the chicken in a
baking dish.
3. Gently separate the skin from the chicken and
stuff the stuffing under the skin. Rub the glaze over
the chicken and place in the preheated oven.
4. Depending on the size of the chicken cook the
bird on Hi about 20 minutes per pound or until the
juices at the thigh run clear.
5. Let the chicken rest for about 10-15 minutes
before carving it.

Chipotle Chicken Burrito
Makes 6 servings
Cook Time: 40 Min

Ingredients
1 pound chicken breast, cubed, boneless, skinless
1 (15 ounce) can black beans, drained and rinsed
1 cup corn, frozen
2 cups tomatoes, crushed
1/2 cup tomato sauce
2 chipotle peppers, canned in adobo sauce, finely
chopped
1/2 teaspoon ground cumin
1/2 salt
2 tablespoon fresh cilantro, chopped
1 clove garlic, minced
3 cups cooked rice
6 flour tortillas, very large

3/4 cup shredded cheddar cheese or pepper jack
cheese
Sour cream

Directions
1. Spray a rectangular glass baking dish with
nonstick cooking spray. Arrange chicken in an even
layer in baking dish.
2. In a bowl combine beans, corn, tomatoes,
chipotle chili peppers, cumin, salt, 1 tablespoon
cilantro and garlic then pour mixture evenly over
chicken. Bake on Hi for 40 minutes.
3. To serve, Heat flour tortillas and put in bowls to
create a tortilla bowls. Divide rice, chicken and
chipolte sauce between bowls. Garnish with
shredded cheese, sour cream and fresh cilantro.

Crumb Coated Chicken
Makes 4 servings
Cook Time: 16 Min

Ingredients
1/2 loaf country bread
1/2 cup parmesan cheese (about 1 1/2 ounces -
freshly grated)
1 tablespoon sage (chopped fresh)
1/4 cup unsalted butter
2 tablespoons Dijon mustard
3/4 lb skinless chicken legs (2 whole)
3/4 lb boneless skinless chicken breast half (2)

Directions
1. Tear bread into pieces and in a food processor
pulse until finely ground. In a large bowl stir
together 2 cups bread crumbs, Parmesan, sage,
and salt and pepper to taste.
2. Melt butter and stir in mustard and salt and
pepper to taste. With a sharp knife cut chicken
thighs from legs. Pat chicken dry and brush all over
with butter mixture.
3. Roll chicken in bread-crumb mixture, pressing
gently to adhere, and arrange chicken, without
crowding, on 4" rack. 7 On level HI, bake chicken
until cooked through and golden, 14 to 16 minutes.

Cumin Chicken
Makes 4 servings
Cook Time: 45 Min

Ingredients
1 3-5lb chicken
2 Tbsp ground cumin
1 Tbsp chopped fresh oregano (or 1 tsp dried oregano)
1 Tbsp fresh ground black pepper
1 Tbsp kosher salt
3 Tbsp white wine
2 Tbsp olive oil

Directions
1. Prepare chicken by cutting off the wing tips. In a small bowl combine the remaining ingredients. Coat the chicken with the mixture inside and out.
2. Push the chicken together so legs and wings are set back. Place the chicken breast side up in a shallow baking dish and set it in the center of Nuwave.
3. Bake on Hi for 45 to an hour. Remove from Nuwave and let it rest for 5 minutes before carving.

Garlic Cheddar Chicken
Makes 2 servings
Cook Time: 30 Min

Ingredients
2 T Butter, melted
1 Clove garlic, minced
3 T Italian style bread crumbs
2 T Parmesan cheese, grated
6 T Colby-Jack cheese, shredded
1/12 t Dried parsley
1/12 t Dried oregano
1/12 t Pepper
1 pinch Salt
2 ea Boneless skinless chicken breast halves (pounded thin)

Directions
1. Melt the butter in a saucepan over low heat, and cook the garlic until tender, about 5 minutes.
2. In a shallow bowl, mix together the Parmesan cheese, shredded Colby-Jack cheese, italian bread crumbs (or plain), parsley, oregano, salt and pepper.
3. Dip each chicken breast in the melted garlic butter to coat, then press into the bread crumb & cheese mixture.
4. Arrange the coated chicken breasts in baking dish. Drizzle with remaining butter and top with any remaining breadcrumbs.

5. Bake on Hi for about 30 minutes or until the chicken is no longer pink and juices run clear.

Garlic Chicken Parmigiana
Makes 5 servings
Cook Time: 20 Min

Ingredients
24 ounces marinara sauce
24 ounces crushed tomatoes
1 tablespoon granulated garlic
1 tablespoon pepper
1 tablespoon basil
4 garlic cloves
1/2 cup onion
1/2 cup chopped mixed mushrooms
1/2 Italian seasoned breadcrumbs
1/4 cup mozzarella cheese
1/4 cup parmigiano-reggiano cheese
12 chicken tenders

Directions
1. Open the jar of marinara sauce, add crushed tomatoes, granulated garlic, pepper, basil. Mix together until well mixed - set aside.
2. Chop onions, mushrooms, garlic. Once chopped add to the sauce and combine. In 2 9 x9 metal pans add about 1/2 - 1 cup marinara sauce add the 6 frozen chicken tenders cover with sauce , ½ the cheese (shredded) parmigiano-reggiano and mozzaella then divide between the two pans. top with 1/2 the bread crumbs on each pan try to cover evenly. (repeat for other pan).
3. In your nuwave cook on Hi 20 minutes or until you feel it is done. (I bake one at a time). If you like it a bit brown(baked cheese) bake for an additional 5 minutes on high.

Grilled Chicken Breast
Cook Time: 16 Min

Ingredients
2 slices prosciutto
1 teaspoon coarse grain mustard
8 fresh basil leaves
1/4 cup mozzarella cheese (grated)
1 whole boneless skinless chicken breast, halved (about 1 pound)

Directions
1. On a work surface spread prosciutto slices evenly with mustard. Top slices with basil leaves and sprinkle evenly with mozzarella.
2. Starting with a short end roll up each prosciutto slice. Pat chicken dry and put on a work surface, skinned sides down. Remove "tender" (fillet strip located on either side of where breast bone was) from each breast half, keeping rest of chicken breast intact, and reserve tenders for another use. (There should be 1 tender from each breast half.).
3. To form a long thin pocket in chicken for prosciutto roll: Put chicken breast halves on cutting board and, beginning at thicker end of breast half, horizontally insert a thin sharp knife three fourths of the way through center of each.
4. Open cut to create a 1-inch-wide pocket in each half. Fit a prosciutto roll into each pocket and season chicken with salt and pepper. Grill chicken on a 4" rack on Nuwave oven until cooked through, about 8 minutes on each side.

Honey and Apricot Baked Chicken
Makes 2 servings
Cook Time: 35 Min

Ingredients
4 chicken drumsticks/thighs
3 tbsp wholegrain mustard
3 tbsp apricot jam
1 tbsp olive oil
1 tsp honey
1 tsp paprika
6 dried apricots to garnish

Directions
1. Mix the honey, oil, mustard and jam. Rub the mixture over the chicken and sprinkle on the paprika.
2. Place the pieces on a lined tray, reserving half of the mixture. Bake for 20 minutes. Turn the chicken over, glaze with the remaining mixture, then return to the oven for another 15 minutes.

Italian Baked Chicken Breast
Makes 2 servings
Cook Time: 25 Min

Ingredients
2 egg whites
2 tsp. balsamic vinegar
1/3 c. dry bread crumbs
1/3 tsp. dried parsley flakes
1/4 tsp. garlic powder
1/4 tsp. garlic salt
2 boneless skinless chicken breast halves (4 oz. each)
butter-flavored cooking spray
1/8 tsp. salt
1/8 tsp. pepper

Directions
1. In a shallow bowl, beat egg whites and vinegar. In another shallow bowl, combine the bread crumbs, parsley, garlic powder and garlic salt.
2. Dip chicken in egg mixture, then coat with crumb mixture. Place in an 8-in. square baking dish coated with cooking spray; lightly coat chicken with butter-flavored spray.
3. Sprinkle with salt and pepper. Bake, uncovered, on Hi for 20-25 mins.

Italian Chicken Rolls
Makes 6 servings
Cook Time: 35 Min

Ingredients
6 (4 oz) skinned, boneless chicken breast halves
1/4 tsp salt
1/4 tsp pepper
1/2 cup chopped roasted red pepper or from a jar
(rinsed and drained)
1/4 cup pesto (homemade or in a jar)
1/3 cup light cream cheese, softened
3/4 cup crushed corn flakes
3 tbsps chopped fresh parsley (or 2 tsp dried)
1/2 tsp paprika
vegetable cooking spray
fresh thyme sprigs (optional)

Directions
1. Place chicken between 2 sheets of heavy-duty
plastic wrap; flatten to 1/4 inch thickness using a
meat mallet. Sprinkle salt and pepper, set aside.
2. Combine red pepper, cream cheese and pesto in
a small bowl, stirring until smooth. Spread cheese
mixture evenly over the chicken breasts. Roll up,
jellyroll fashion, secure with wooden picks.
3. Dredge chicken pieces in combined corn flakes,
parsley and paprika. Place in a baking dish coated
with cooking spray. Bake on Hi, uncovered, for 35
minutes.
4. Let stand 10 minutes and remove tooth picks.
Slice each roll into 6 rounds or slices for each
person. Garnish with thyme sprigs if desired.

Italian Chicken Strips
Makes 2 servings
Cook Time: 18 Min

Ingredients
6 -8 chicken strips (Frozen)
2 eggs, slightly beaten and mixed with small
amount of milk
1/2 cup cracker crumb (Crushed)
1/2 cup Italian breadcrumbs (seasoned)
1 dash salt or 1 dash pepper, and or 1 dash garlic
powder

Directions
1. Combine the cracker crumbs, bread crumbs and
spices in a Ziploc bag. (add any spices you wish).
Dredge the frozen chicken strips in the egg/milk
mixture and then drop into the ziploc with the
cracker/spice mixture.

2. Shake well to coat the chicken strips. Place
chicken in a baking dish (that will fit into the
NuWave oven) that has been sprayed with Pam.
3. Set NuWave oven to cook for 9 minutes at power
9. Turn chicken over and continue cooking for
another 9 minutes.

Lemon Pepper Chicken
Makes 4 servings
Cook Time:30 Min

Ingredients
4 frozen boneless skinless chicken breast halves
1/2 cup crushed cracker crumb
2 medium lemons
1 dash fresh ground pepper
1 dash salt
1 bunch fresh asparagus
1 tablespoon oil

Directions
1. Clean & prepare your asparagus, place in a bowl
and pour oil or melted butter on top, sprinkle with
salt and toss, set aside.
2. Zest both lemons and mix the zest with the
cracker crumbs. Cut the lemons in half. Place the
frozen chicken breasts on the rack.
3. Squeeze one lemon half over the top of all the
chicken breasts. Sprinkle with salt. Cover the top of
each chicken breast with about a 1/4 inch layer of
cracker crumbs, press down.
4. Squeeze another lemon half over the crumbs
then add freshly ground pepper (you can add as
much or little as you like).
5. Heat on high for 15 minutes or until the crumbs
begin to brown (add more time if necessary). Turn
chicken breasts over and repeat.
6. Add the asparagus to the bottom platter, replace
the chicken on the rack over the asparagus. Cook
on high for another 15 minutes or until the crumbs
are browned and the asparagus is done.

Mustard Chicken
Cook Time: 16 Min

Ingredients
1 chicken breast
3 large lemons, juice of
2 tablespoons Dijon mustard
2 tablespoons garlic
1 teaspoon cajun seasoning
1 teaspoon thyme
1 teaspoon sage
1 teaspoon rosemary

Directions

1. Combine the above ingredients and marinate the chicken breast in it for 1-3 hours.
2. Toss on the NuWave rack and cook until tender and juicy. (About 6-8 minutes per side).

Oven Fried Chicken
Makes 6 servings
Cook Time: 45 Min

Ingredients
½ cup dry bread crumbs
1 cup grated Parmesan cheese
½ tsp. paprika
¼ tsp. ground black pepper
2 eggs, lightly beaten
1 tbsp. water
3 lbs. boneless, skinless chicken breast halves (about 6 medium-to-small)

Directions
1. Spray foil with nonstick cooking spray. In a large bowl, combine bread crumbs, Parmesan cheese, paprika and black pepper; mix well. In a small bowl, whisk together eggs and water.
2. Dip chicken pieces into egg mixture, and then roll in bread crumb mixture. Put chicken pieces on baking sheet.
3. Bake on Hi for 45 minutes to 1 hour, or until meat is no longer pink and juices run clear.

Oven Fried Chicken Breasts
Makes 2 servings
Cook Time: 40 Min

Ingredients
1/4 cup dry bread crumbs
1 tbsp. grated parmesan cheese
1 tsp. paprika
1 tsp. dried thyme
1/2 tsp. garlic
1/4 tsp. pepper
1/3 cup buttermilk
4 skinned chicken breasts
Cooking spray
1 tbsp butter, melted

Directions
1. Combine bread crumbs, parm cheese, paprika, thyme, salt and pepper in shallow dish. Dip chicken in buttermilk and dredge in bread crumb mixture.

2. Spray pan with the cooking spray. Place chicken, breast sides up in pan. Drizzle melted butter over chicken. Bake on Hi for 40 minutes or until done.

Red Wine Garlic Chicken
Makes 4 servings
Cook Time: 40 Min

Ingredients
4 boneless skinless chicken breast
4 cloves of garlic minced
1 Tbsp taragon
salt 2 pinches
pepper 2 pinches
1/4-1/2 bottle red wine depends on your pan

Directions
1. place chicken in a baking dish then sprinkle with salt, pepper, garlic and taragon.
2. Fill up pan with wine so that 1/2 of the chicken breast are covered.
3. Cover and bake on Hi until done approx. 40min.

Roasted Chicken
Makes 5 servings
Cook Time: 2-3 Hrs

Ingredients
1 -10 lb. oven stuffer chicken
Handful of Italian parsley - chopped
Handful of cilantro . chopped
5 cloves of garlic . chopped
1- Tablespoon of capers . plus tablespoon of caper juice
1 cup of pepper and sea salt croutons . crushed coarsely (or your preferred flavor)
¼ cup of olive oil
¼ cup of olive oil
Dashes of paprika
Dash o f chili powder
1 tsp of dried oregano
Dashes of black pepper
Juice of ½ lemon

Directions
1. Wash bird inside and out and pat dry. Combine all of the ingredients for the stuffing and mix well.
2. Gently separate the skin from the meat of the chicken and stuff the mixture under the skin.
3. Combine the ingredients for the rub and smooth the rub all over the skin of the chicken. Place in a baking dish and bake on Hi until the skin is golden and the juices run clear.

Smoked Turkey Quesadillas
Makes 2 servings
Cook Time: 5 Min

Ingredients
2 flour tortillas
1/4 cup Velveeta cheese, chopped into small chunks
1/2 cup smoked turkey (sliced)
1/3 cup canned diced green chiles
1/4 cup sour cream

Directions
1. Brush 2 tortillas with oil. Place tortillas, oil side down, on baking sheet. Sprinkle each with 1/4 of cheese, half of turkey, half of cheese, and half of the chilies, leaving 3/4-inch border.
2. Top each with 1 tortilla, pressing to adhere; brush top with oil. Bake quesadillas until filling is heated through and edges begin to crisp, about 2~3 minutes.
3. Using large metal spatula, turn each over and bake until bottom is crisp, about 1~2 minutes.
4. Transfer quesadillas to plates. Cut into wedges and serve. Top with Sour Cream. You can use a spicy version of Velveta as well.

Spicy Chicken Wings
Makes 4 servings
Cook Time: 20 Min

Ingredients
1 1/2 teaspoons minced garlic
1 1/2 teaspoons Chinese five spice powder
1 1/4 teaspoons salt
1 1/2 teaspoons soy sauce
3 lbs chicken wings (about 16)

Directions
1. Stir together garlic, five-spice powder, salt, and soy sauce in a large bowl. Cut off and discard tips from chicken wings with kitchen shears or a large heavy knife, then halve wings at joint.
2. Pat dry and add to spice mixture, tossing to coat. Arrange wings in nuwave oven pan and heat on 4 inch rack, turning over once, until browned and cooked through, 18 to 20 minutes total.

Teriyaki Chicken
Makes 4 servings
Cook Time: 15 Min

Ingredients
3 -4 boneless chicken breasts
1/2 cup teriyaki marinade, sauce

1 medium onion
1 tablespoon chopped garlic
1 tablespoon lemon juice
1 teaspoon pepper

Directions
1. Cut chicken breasts into 3 to 4 inch pieces. Place in a zip-loc bag along with Teriyaki Sauce, diced onion, garlic, lemon juice and pepper. Marinate in the refrigerator for 2 hours.
2. Place Chicken on the 1 inch rack in the Nu-wave Oven and cook for 15 minutes. Pour Teriyaki Marinade into an aluminum pan, casserole dish, or any container that can be placed in the Nu-wave Oven.
3. Remove chicken from the oven and place it on top of the marinade. Be sure to turn it over. Cook for 15 minutes. Let it sit for 5-10 minutes and serve.

Thai Basil Chicken
Makes 6 servings
Cook Time: 55 Min

Ingredients
2 Tbs fish sauce or substitute soy sauce
2 Tbs light soy sauce
2 Tbs plain low fat yogurt
Juice and grated peel of 1 lemon
3 cloves garlic, minced
3 Tbs minced fresh basil or 1 tsp dried basil
2 tsp hot red pepper flakes
1 tsp ground ginger
3 lbs chicken thighs, trimmed of fat

Directions
1. Put all ingredients except chicken in a plastic bag and knead to mix. Add chicken and turn bag to coat pieces.
2. Marinate at room temperature for 30 minutes or for several hours in refrigerator. Remove chicken from bag and arrange, skin side up, in a shallow roasting pan.
3. Bake on Hi for 55 minutes or until juices run clear.

Thyme Turkey Breast
Makes 6 servings
Cook Time: 1 Hr 30 Min

Ingredients
4 lbs turkey breast, Frozen
3 tablespoons rosemary
3 tablespoons thyme
2 1/2 tablespoons garlic salt (or regular salt if you like)

Directions
1. Mix Rosemary, Thyme & garlic salt together. Dunk Turkey Breast in warm water for a minute or two. This will make the skin able to take rub.
2. Place rub all over Turkey. Place in your Nuwave for 1 1/2 to 1 3/4 hours on high. If Turkey starts to get brown, you can "flip it over" 3/4 of the way though cooking time. This will brown both sides of the Turkey.
3. If you wish to cook one side, cover with foil if getting to brown. Check Turkey with therm. It should read 180 for well done, if lower cook an additional 10 minute Check again.

Turkey Bacon
Makes 4 servings
Cook Time: 13 Min

Ingredients
8 slices turkey bacon
1 dash pepper

Directions
1. Cook on 4 inch cooking rack for 12-13 minutes or until it looks done to your liking. Normally I like mine very crispy.

Turkey Enchiladas
Makes 8 servings
Cook Time: 20 Min

Ingredients
1 1/2 lbs ground turkey (can use one pound if that is all that is avail)
1 onion (med-chopped)
16 ounces olives (whole or sliced)
16 ounces light sour cream
6 -8 flour tortillas (burrito size)
2 -3 cups cheese (shredded)
1 (20 ounce) can red enchilada sauce (med or mild)
1 (10 3/4 ounce) can campbell's tomato soup (undiluted)
1 (1 1/4 ounce) package taco seasoning

Directions
1. Brown ground turkey & onions in pan (in oil). Sprinkle contentions of pkg. over meat. Add 1 ½ cup water and simmer for 5 minutes. Keep warm.
2. To assemble: mixed tomato soup and enchilada cause together in a bowl. 1 tortilla on a plate, take a tbsp of sauce and spread over tortilla. Take meat and put ½ cup meat down middle.
3. On top of that put cheese on top. Then add olives on top of that. 2 tablespoons sour cream on pile.
4. Roll up and put seam face down in 9 x 13 pan. Make sure you put sauce down on bottom of pan first. Then add enchiladas. Continue until full. Make sure you have enough sauce & cheese at the end.
5. Cook on HI heat for 15 - 20 minutes or until Cheese if melted and looks done.

Seafood

Asian Salmon I
Makes 2 servings

Ingredients
12 ounces salmon fillets
3 tablespoons hoisin sauce
3 tablespoons soy sauce
4 slices fresh ginger or 1/2 teaspoon ground ginger
2 garlic cloves, finely chopped
1 teaspoon sesame oil
1 dash sesame seed
5 asparagus spears

Directions
1. Mix hoisen, soy, ginger, and garlic. Place half of mixture on plate and place salmon, skin side up on mixture. Refrigerate for 1/2 hour.
2. Spray cooking rack with non-stick spray and place filets skin side down on 4" rack. Baste once more with left over mixture on top and sides.
3. Nu-Wave on HI for 5 minutes. Meanwhile, lightly brush asparagus with sesame oil and sprinkle on sesame seeds.
4. Place around salmon on 4" rack and continue for 5 more minutes (or until both are done.

Asian Salmon II
Makes 8 servings
Cook Time: 30 Min

Ingredients
2 pounds salmon filets, with skin
2 tablespoons olive oil
2 tablespoons rice vinegar
2 tablespoons soy sauce
1 tablespoon packed brown sugar
2 cloves garlic, minced
1 pinch ground black pepper
2 tablespoons minced onion
1 tablespoon sesame oil
2 cups long-grain white rice
1 teaspoon dried dill weed
4 cups water

Directions
1. Make several shallow slashes in the skinless side of the salmon filets. Place filets skin-side down in a glass baking dish.
2. In a medium bowl, whisk together the olive oil, rice vinegar, soy sauce, brown sugar, garlic, pepper, onion and sesame oil.

3. Pour the liquid over the salmon, cover and refrigerate for 1 to 2 hours. In a medium saucepan combine the rice, water and dillweed.
4. Bring to a boil, then cook over medium low heat until rice is tender and water has been absorbed, about 20 minutes.
5. Remove cover from salmon, and bake in the marinating dish on Hi for about 30 minutes, or until fish can be flaked with a fork. Serve salmon over the rice, and pour sauce over.

Baked Haddock
Makes 4 servings
Cook Time: 15 Min

Ingredients
3/4 cup milk
2 teaspoons salt
3/4 cup bread crumbs
1/4 cup grated Parmesan cheese
1/4 teaspoon ground dried thyme
4 haddock fillets
1/4 cup butter, melted

Directions
1. In a small bowl, combine the milk and salt. In a separate bowl, mix together the bread crumbs, parmesan cheese, and thyme.
2. Dip the haddock fillets in the milk, then press into the crumb mixture to coat. Place haddock fillets in a glass baking dish, and drizzle with melted butter.
3. Bake on Hi until the fish flakes easily, about 15 minutes.

Baked Seafood Au Gratin
Makes 8 servings
Cook Time: 1 Hr

Ingredients
1 onion, chopped
1 green bell pepper, chopped
1 cup butter, divided
1 cup all-purpose flour, divided
1 pound fresh crabmeat
4 cups water
1 pound fresh shrimp, peeled and deveined
1/2 pound small scallops
1/2 pound flounder fillets
3 cups milk
1 cup shredded sharp Cheddar cheese
1 tablespoon distilled white vinegar
1 teaspoon Worcestershire sauce
1/2 teaspoon salt
1 pinch ground black pepper
1 dash hot pepper sauce
1/2 cup grated Parmesan cheese

Directions
1. In a heavy skillet, saute the onion and the pepper in 1/2 cup of butter. Cook until tender. Mix in 1/2 cup of the flour, and cook over medium heat for 10 minutes, stirring frequently. Stir in crabmeat, remove from heat, and set aside.
2. In a large Dutch oven, bring the water to a boil. Add the shrimp, scallops, and flounder, and simmer for 3 minutes. Drain, reserving 1 cup of the cooking liquid, and set the seafood aside.
3. In a heavy saucepan, melt the remaining 1/2 cup butter over low heat. Stir in remaining 1/2 cup flour. Cook and stir constantly for 1 minute.
4. Gradually add the milk plus the 1 cup reserved cooking liquid. Raise heat to medium; cook, stirring constantly, until the mixture is thickened and bubbly.
5. Mix in the shredded Cheddar cheese, vinegar, Worcestershire sauce, salt, pepper, and hot sauce. Stir in cooked seafood.
6. Lightly grease baking dish. Press crabmeat mixture into the bottom of the prepared pan. Spoon the seafood mixture over the crabmeat crust, and sprinkle with the Parmesan cheese.
7. Bake on Hi for 30 minutes, or until lightly browned. Serve immediately.

Baked Swordfish
Makes 4 servings

Ingredients
1/3 cup oil-cured green olives, chopped pitted
1/3 cup oil-cured black olive, chopped pitted (such as Kalamata)
1/4 cup roasted red pepper, from jars, chopped
1 tablespoon parsley, minced fresh
2 anchovy fillets, minced
2 teaspoons capers, drained
1 teaspoon red wine vinegar
1 large garlic clove, minced
3 tablespoons olive oil

Directions

1. 4 6-ounce swordfish steaks (about 3/4 inch thick). Combine all olives, roasted peppers, parsley, minced anchovies, capers, vinegar and garlic in small bowl.
2. Stir in 1 tablespoon olive oil. Season with salt and pepper. Let stand 1 hour. (Can be made 1 day ahead. Cover and chill.
3. Serve at room temperature. Place swordfish steaks on a 4" rack. Brush swordfish on both sides with remaining 2 tablespoons olive oil. Season with salt and pepper.
4. Bake on HI just until fish is cooked through, about 5 minutes per side. Transfer to platter. Spoon olive relish over swordfish and serve.

Barbequed Shrimp
Makes 45 servings

Ingredients
3 lbs large shrimp, about 45, shelled, leaving the tails intact, butterflied, and deveined
2 cups spicy tomato base barbecue sauce

Directions
1. Insert a 10-inch bamboo skewer at the tail end of each shrimp and thread the shrimp onto it. Brush the shrimp with the barbecue sauce and arrange them on a 4" rack.
2. Just before grilling brush the shrimp again with the sauce, grill them on High for 2~3 minutes on each side, or until they are pink and springy to the touch, and serve them warm or at room temperature.

Buttered Lobster

Ingredients
2 lbs lobsters
3 tablespoons butter
1 dash salt and pepper
1 dash lemon juice

Directions

1. Remove lobster meat from shell and chop in cubes. Melt butter. In a shallow baking dish add lobster melted butter, lemon juice and salt & pepper.
2. Bake for 10 to 12 minutes. 5 Serve with lemon wedges.

Cajun Crab Stuffed Mushrooms
Makes 4 servings
Cook Time: 10 Min

Ingredients
1 (8 ounce) package cream cheese, softened
1/2 cup shredded Colby-Monterey Jack cheese
1 teaspoon seafood seasoning (such as Old Bay®)
1/2 teaspoon Cajun seasoning
1/4 teaspoon cayenne hot pepper sauce, or to taste (optional)
1/4 teaspoon garlic powder
1 (8 ounce) package imitation crabmeat, flaked
1/4 cup Italian seasoned bread crumbs
1 (8 ounce) package crimini mushrooms, stems removed

Directions
1. Grease a 9x5 inch baking dish. Stir the cream cheese, Colby-Monterey Jack cheese, seafood seasoning, Cajun seasoning, hot pepper sauce, and garlic powder in a mixing bowl until smooth.
2. Stir in the crabmeat and bread crumbs until evenly blended. Spoon the cheese mixture into the mushroom caps; set them filling-side-up into the prepared baking dish.
3. Bake on Hi for 7 minutes; set the oven to broil and broil until the tops are crisp and brown, about 3 minutes.

Crab and Shrimp
Makes 4 servings

Ingredients
1 bell pepper (chopped)
1 onion (chopped)
1 stalk celery (chopped)
1 teaspoon Lea & Perrins Worcestershire Sauce
8 -10 ounces crabmeat
1 lb shrimp
1 dash salt
1 dash pepper
1 cup mayonnaise
1/4 cup potato chip

Directions

1. Mix all ingredients except the potato chip, place in baking dish. Crush potato chips and sprinkle on top of mixture. Bake 15 to 18 minutes.

Crab Crusted Grouper
Makes 4 servings
Cook Time: 30 Min

Ingredients
2 tablespoons Parmesan cheese flavored bread crumbs
2 tablespoons chopped red bell pepper
2 tablespoons chopped yellow bell pepper
2 green onions, chopped
1/4 jalapeno pepper, seeded and minced
4 tablespoons butter, melted
1 (6 ounce) can crabmeat, drained and flaked
2 tablespoons shredded mozzarella cheese
4 (6 ounce) fillets grouper

Directions
1. In a medium bowl, stir together the bread crumbs, red pepper, yellow pepper, green onions, jalapeno, butter, crabmeat, and mozzarella cheese.
2. Arrange grouper fillets in a single layer in a baking dish. Spread the crumb topping evenly over the fish.
3. Bake on Hi for 30 minutes or until fish is easily flaked with a fork. If you have thin fillets, you may broil for 10 minutes instead of baking.

Crawfish Fettuccine
Makes 8 servings
Cook Time: 1 Hr 15 Min

Ingredients
6 tablespoons butter
1 large onion, chopped
1 green bell pepper, chopped
3 stalks celery, chopped
1 clove garlic, minced
1 tablespoon all-purpose flour
1 pound peeled crawfish tails
1 (8 ounce) package processed cheese food
1 cup half-and-half cream
2 teaspoons Cajun seasoning
2 teaspoons cayenne pepper
1 pound dry fettuccine pasta
1/2 cup grated Parmesan cheese

Directions
1. Melt the butter in a large skillet over medium heat. Cook onion, bell pepper, celery, and garlic in butter until onions are tender. Stir in flour, and cook for 5 to 10 minutes, stirring frequently. Stir in crawfish. Cover, and simmer for 15 to 20 minutes, stirring often.
2. Stir in the processed cheese, half-and-half, Cajun seasonings, and cayenne pepper. Cover, and simmer for about 20 minutes, stirring occasionally.
3. Meanwhile, bring a large pot of lightly salted water to a boil. Cook pasta in boiling water for 8 to 10 minutes, or until al dente; drain.
4. Butter a baking dish. Stir noodles into crawfish mixture; pour into prepared dish, and sprinkle with Parmesan cheese. 5. Bake on Hi for 20 minutes, or until hot and bubbly.

Crusted Salmon with Honey-Mustard Sauce
Makes 4 servings
Cook Time: 15 Min

Ingredients
1 (1.5 pound) skinless center-cut salmon fillet, cut into 4 pieces
1 cup milk
1/4 cup fine bread crumbs
2 tablespoons grated Parmesan cheese
1 egg
1/4 cup butter, melted
1 tablespoon prepared yellow mustard
1 tablespoon honey

Directions
1. Prepare a baking sheet with cooking spray.
2. Place the salmon fillets in a baking dish; pour the milk over the fillets. Allow the salmon to soak in the milk 10 to 15 minutes.
3. Stir the bread crumbs and Parmesan cheese together in a wide, deep bowl. Beat the egg in a separate bowl until frothy. Remove the salmon fillets from the milk; shake the excess milk off the fish. Dip each fillet into the beaten egg and then gently press into the bread crumb mixture to coat; gently shake to remove the excess.
4. Bake on Hi, turning once, until the salmon flakes easily with a fork, about 15 minutes.
5. While the salmon bakes, stir the butter, mustard, and honey together in a bowl; drizzle over the baked salmon to serve.

Garlic Alfredo Tilapia
Makes 4 servings
Cook Time: 15 Min

Ingredients
4 tilapia fillets
2 tablespoons olive oil
1 tablespoon Creole seasoning, or to taste
3 tablespoons butter
2 cloves garlic, minced
1 cup Alfredo sauce

Directions
1. Brush the tilapia fillets with oil on both sides, season with Creole seasoning to taste, then place into a baking dish.
2. Bake on Hi until the flesh is no longer translucent, and the fish flakes easily with a fork, about 10 minutes.
3. Meanwhile, melt the butter in a small saucepan over medium heat. Stir in the garlic, and cook until the garlic has softened and the aroma has mellowed, about 2 minutes. Stir in the Alfredo sauce and bring to a simmer.
4. Reduce the heat to low, and keep warm until the fish is ready. Pour the sauce over the fish to serve. Sprinkle with additional Creole seasoning if desired.

Goat Cheese and Shrimp Pizza
Makes 2 servings

Ingredients
1/2 cup chopped red onion
1 1/2 cups olives, chopped
1/2 cup goat cheese
1 cup mozzarella cheese (grated)
14 ounces pizza crusts (Store bought)
3/4 cup barbecue sauce
1/2 cup shrimp
1 tablespoon Old Bay Seasoning

Directions
1. Spread Barbeque sauce onto store bought pizza crust. Sprinkle on goat cheese.
2. Add shrimp, chopped olives and red onions. Top with shredded cheese of your choice.
3. Sprinkle Old Bay Seasoning on top of pizza.
4. Bake on Hi heat for 10 - 13 minutes or until brown and cooked though.

Greek-Style Baked Salmon
Makes 8 servings
Cook Time: 20 Min

Ingredients
8 (5 ounce) salmon fillets, with skin
1/4 cup olive oil
4 plum tomatoes, diced
1/2 cup crumbled feta cheese
1/4 red onion, diced
1 tablespoon chopped fresh basil
4 kalamata olives, sliced
1 tablespoon lemon juice

Directions
1. Brush each salmon fillet on all sides with olive oil and arrange into the bottom of a glass baking dish with the skin side facing down.
2. Scatter the tomatoes, feta cheese, onion, basil, and olives over the fillets; sprinkle with the lemon juice.
3. Bake on Hi until the salmon flakes easily with a fork, about 20 minutes.

Grilled Salmon
Makes 2 servings

Ingredients
3 tablespoons packed dark brown sugar
4 teaspoons prepared Chinese hot mustard or 4 teaspoons Dijon mustard
1 tablespoon soy sauce
1 teaspoon rice vinegar

2 (7 -8 ounce) salmon steaks (about 3/4-inch thick)

Directions
1. Combine brown sugar, mustard and soy sauce in medium bowl; whisk to blend. Transfer 1 tablespoon glaze to small bowl; mix in rice vinegar and set aside.
2. Brush 1 side of salmon steaks generously with half of glaze in medium bowl. Place salmon steaks, glazed side down, onto 4" rack.
3. Grill about 4 minutes. Brush top side of salmon steaks with remaining glaze in medium bowl.
4. Turn salmon over and grill until second side is just opaque in center, about 4 minutes. Transfer salmon to plates. Drizzle reserved glaze in small bowl over salmon and serve.

Halibut Steaks
Makes 4 servings
Cook Time: 15 Min

Ingredients
1 teaspoon olive oil
1 cup diced zucchini
1/2 cup minced onion
1 clove garlic, peeled and minced
2 cups diced fresh tomatoes
2 tablespoons chopped fresh basil
1/4 teaspoon salt
1/4 teaspoon ground black pepper
4 (6 ounce) halibut steaks
1/3 cup crumbled feta cheese

Directions
1. Lightly grease a shallow baking dish.
2. Heat olive oil in a medium saucepan over medium heat and stir in zucchini, onion, and garlic. Cook and stir 5 minutes or until tender. Remove saucepan from heat and mix in tomatoes, basil, salt, and pepper.
3. Arrange halibut steaks in a single layer in the prepared baking dish. Spoon equal amounts of the zucchini mixture over each steak. Top with feta cheese.
4. Bake 15 minutes on Hi, or until fish is easily flaked with a fork.

Herbed Salmon Steaks
Makes 4 servings
Cook Time: 30 Min

Ingredients
1/4 cup butter or margarine, melted
2/3 cup crushed saltine crackers
1/4 cup grated Parmesan cheese
1/2 teaspoon salt
1/2 teaspoon dried basil
1/2 teaspoon dried oregano
1/4 teaspoon garlic powder
4 (6 ounce) salmon steaks

Directions
1. Place butter in a shallow dish. In another dish, combine the cracker crumbs, Parmesan cheese, salt, basil, oregano and garlic powder.
2. Dip salmon into butter, then coat both sides with crumb mixture. Place in a greased baking dish. Bake on Hi for 30-35 minutes or until fish flakes easily with a fork.

Honey-Orange Marinated Salmon
Makes 4 servings
Cook Time: 30 Min

Ingredients
1/3 cup reduced-sodium soy sauce
1/4 cup orange juice
1/4 cup honey
2 green onions, thinly sliced
1 tablespoon olive oil
1 tablespoon sherry or apple juice
1 tablespoon minced fresh ginger root
1 pound salmon fillet

Directions
1. In a large resealable plastic bag, combine the first seven ingredients. Add salmon. Seal bag and turn to coat; refrigerate for 1 hour, turning several times.
2. Line a square baking dish with foil; coat the foil with nonstick cooking spray. Drain and discard marinade. Place salmon in prepared pan. Bake on Hi for 30-40 minutes or until fish flakes easily with a fork.

Salmon Loaf
Makes 2 servings
Cook Time: 40 Min

Ingredients
3/4 cup chopped celery
1/2 cup chopped onion
2 tablespoons vegetable oil
1 (7 ounce) can salmon, drained, bones and skin removed
1 egg, lightly beaten
2 tablespoons milk
1 cup soft bread crumbs
1/4 teaspoon salt
1/4 teaspoon pepper
1/2 cup mayonnaise
1/4 cup sour cream
1 tablespoon lemon juice
1 tablespoon milk
2 teaspoons snipped fresh dill
1/2 teaspoon sugar
1/8 teaspoon pepper

Directions
1. In a skillet, saute celery and onion in oil until tender. In a bowl, combine the salmon, egg, milk, bread crumbs, salt, pepper and celery mixture. Transfer to a greased loaf pan.
2. Bake on Hi for 40-45 minutes or until a knife inserted near the center comes our clean. In a small bowl, combine the sauce ingredients. Serve with salmon loaf.

Salmon with Brown Sugar
Makes 4 servings
Cook Time: 10 Min

Ingredients
1/4 cup packed light brown sugar
2 tablespoons Dijon mustard
4 (6 ounce) boneless salmon fillets
salt and ground black pepper to taste

Directions
1. Season the salmon with salt and pepper and arrange onto the prepared broiler pan. Whisk together the brown sugar and Dijon mustard in a small bowl; spoon mixture evenly onto top of salmon fillets.
2. Cook on Hi until the fish flakes easily with a fork, 10 to 15 minutes.

Seafood Alfredo Lasagna
Makes 12 servings
Cook Time: 1 Hr 30 Min

Ingredients
1 (16 ounce) package lasagna noodles
2 tablespoons olive oil
1 clove garlic, minced
1 pound baby portobello mushrooms, sliced
32 ounces Classico® Creamy Alfredo Sauce
1 pound shrimp, peeled and deveined
1 pound bay scallops
1 pound imitation crabmeat, chopped
20 ounces ricotta cheese
1 egg
black pepper
6 cups shredded Italian cheese blend

Directions
1. Bring a large pot of lightly salted water to a boil. Add pasta and cook for 8 to 10 minutes or until al dente; drain.
2. Heat oil in a large saucepan over medium heat. Cook and stir garlic and mushrooms until tender. Pour in 2 jars Alfredo sauce. Stir in shrimp, scallops and crabmeat. Simmer 5 to 10 minutes, or until heated through. In a medium
bowl, combine ricotta cheese, egg and pepper.
3. In a baking dish, layer noodles, ricotta mixture, Alfredo mixture and shredded cheese. Repeat layers until all ingredients are used, ensuring that there is shredded cheese for the top.
4. Bake on Hi for 45 minutes. Cover, and bake 15 minutes.

Seafood Au Gratin
Makes 8 servings
Cook Time: 15 Min

Ingredients
2 tablespoons olive oil
1 pound fresh shrimp, peeled and deveined
1 pound bay or sea scallops, rinsed and drained
3 tablespoons butter
2 tablespoons all-purpose flour
2 cups hot chicken broth
3 tablespoons chopped shallots
1 (4 ounce) can button mushrooms, drained
1/2 cup white wine
1 pound cooked crab meat
2 cups shredded provolone cheese
1/2 cup grated Parmesan cheese
2 tablespoons chopped fresh parsley

Directions
1. Lightly butter 8 small baking dishes.
2. In a large skillet, heat olive oil over medium high heat. Saute shrimp and scallops until firm, about 5 minutes.
3. In a medium saucepan, melt butter over medium heat. Stir in flour until smooth. Gradually add chicken broth and raise heat to high. Stir until thickened. Mix in shallots, mushrooms and wine. Cook for 5 to 10 minutes.
4. Arrange shrimp, scallops and crab in the bottom of prepared dishes. Pour sauce over seafood and cover with cheese.
5. Bake on Hi until golden, about 12 t o15 minutes. Sprinkle with parsley and serve.

Seafood Bake for Two
Makes 2 servings
Cook Time: 10 Min

Ingredients
2 (4 ounce) halibut fillets
6 scallops
6 peeled and deveined jumbo shrimp, tail still attached
1/3 cup dry white wine
2 tablespoons melted butter
1 tablespoon lemon juice
1/2 teaspoon seafood seasoning, such as Old Bay.
1 teaspoon minced garlic
Salt and pepper to taste
1 tablespoon chopped fresh parsley

Directions
1. Arrange the halibut, scallops, and shrimp in an oven-safe, glass baking dish.
2. Drizzle with wine, butter, and lemon juice. Sprinkle with the seasoning and garlic. Season to taste with salt and pepper.
3. Bake on Hi until the halibut has turned white, and is flaky, 10 to 12 minutes. Sprinkle with parsley just before serving.

Seafood Egg Rolls
Makes 12 servings
Cook Time: 15 Min

Ingredients
1/4 pound bay scallops
1/4 pound medium shrimp, peeled and deveined
1 teaspoon minced garlic, divided
2 tablespoons olive or vegetable oil, divided
1 large tomato - peeled, seeded and chopped
1/4 cup finely chopped onion
3 tablespoons minced fresh parsley
3 tablespoons minced fresh cilantro or additional parsley
3/4 teaspoon ground cumin
1/2 teaspoon paprika
1/4 teaspoon salt
1/8 teaspoon pepper
dash cayenne pepper
1 pinch ground turmeric
1/4 cup soft bread crumbs
8 ounces phyllo dough, thawed
1/2 cup butter or margarine, melted

Directions
1. In a large skillet, saute scallops, shrimp and 1/2 teaspoon garlic in 1 tablespoon oil for 2 minutes or until seafood is opaque. With a slotted spoon, remove from the pan and coarsely chop; set aside. In the same skillet, combine the tomato, onion and remaining garlic and oil; simmer for 5 minutes.
2. Stir in parsley, cilantro, cumin, paprika, salt, pepper, cayenne and turmeric. Simmer, uncovered, until liquid is evaporated, about 5 minutes. Stir in seafood mixture and bread crumbs. 2. Cut the phyllo dough into 14-in. x 4-1/2-in. strips.
3. Cover with a damp towel until ready to use. Lightly brush one strip with butter. Top with another strip; brush with butter. Place a tablespoonful of seafood mixture near one short side; fold in the long sides and roll up.
4. Brush lightly with butter. Place on a greased baking sheet. Repeat with remaining phyllo and filling. Bake on Hi for 12-15 minutes or until golden brown.

Seafood Nachos
Makes 6 servings
Cook Time: 10 Min

Ingredients
30 baked tortilla chips
1 (8 ounce) package imitation crabmeat, chopped
1/4 cup reduced-fat sour cream
1/4 cup reduced-fat mayonnaise
2 tablespoons finely chopped onion
1/4 teaspoon dill weed
1 cup shredded reduced-fat Cheddar cheese
1/4 cup sliced ripe olives
1/4 teaspoon paprika

Directions
1. Arrange tortilla chips in a single layer on an ungreased baking sheet. In a bowl, combine the crab, sour cream, mayonnaise, onion and dill; spoon about 1 tablespoon onto each chip.
2. Sprinkle with cheese, olives and paprika. Bake on Hi for 6-8 minutes or until cheese is melted.

Seafood Pot Pie
Makes 4 servings
Cook Time: 40 Min

Ingredients
1/2 (17.3 ounce) package Pepperidge Farm® Puff Pastry Sheets
Vegetable cooking spray
1 (10.75 ounce) can Campbell's® Condensed Cream of Onion Soup
1 (10.75 ounce) can Campbell's® Condensed New England Clam Chowder
1/2 cup milk
1/8 teaspoon hot pepper sauce
1 (10 ounce) package frozen mixed vegetables, thawed
1 (12 ounce) bag frozen cooked baby shrimp, thawed
1 (6 ounce) can imitation crabmeat (surimi)

Directions
1. Thaw the pastry at room temperature for 40 minutes or until it's easy to handle. Spray a shallow baking dish with cooking spray.
2. Stir the soups, milk, hot sauce, vegetables, shrimp and crabmeat into the prepared dish.
3. Unfold the pastry sheet on a lightly floured surface. Roll the sheet into a 10 x 9-inch rectangle. Gently roll the pastry onto the rolling pin so that you can lift it and gently unroll it on the baking dish. Crimp or roll the edges to seal it to the dish.
4. Bake on Hi for 40 minutes or until the pastry is golden brown and the filling is hot and bubbling. Let the pot pie stand for 5 minutes before serving.

Seafood Quiche
Makes 6 servings
Cook Time: 30 Min

Ingredients
6 ounces crabmeat
1/2 cup bread crumbs
1/2 cup milk
2 eggs, beaten
2 tablespoons chopped fresh parsley
1 tablespoon lemon juice
1 teaspoon prepared mustard
1/4 teaspoon Worcestershire sauce
salt to taste
ground black pepper to taste
1 pinch cayenne pepper
1 pinch paprika

Directions
1. Lightly grease a 9 inch pie pan.
2. Pick through the crab meat and remove any bits of shell or cartilage.
3. In a medium mixing bowl, combine crabmeat, bread crumbs, milk, eggs, parsley, lemon juice, mustard, Worcestershire sauce, salt, pepper and cayenne pepper. Transfer the quiche mixture to the prepared pan. Sprinkle paprika over the quiche.
4. Bake on Hi for 30 minutes, or until the quiche is firm in the center.

Seafood Strata with Pesto
Makes 8 servings
Cook Time: 1 Hr

Ingredients
12 slices day-old sourdough bread, crusts removed
1 cup basil pesto
3 tablespoons butter
1 (10 ounce) package sliced fresh mushrooms
1 cup chopped green onion
1/4 cup dry sherry
8 ounces medium shrimp - peeled and deveined
8 ounces fresh crabmeat
2 cups shredded Swiss cheese
6 eggs
3 cups half-and-half cream
1/2 teaspoon salt
1/8 teaspoon cayenne pepper
1/2 cup panko bread crumbs
1 medium tomato, cut into wedges
1 tablespoon chopped fresh basil or chives for garnish

Directions
1. Cut each slice of bread into 4 triangles. Place them on a baking sheet, and bake for about 10 minutes, or until toasted. Allow to cool, then spread pesto onto one side of each piece of bread. Set aside.
2. Melt the butter in a large skillet over medium heat. Add the mushrooms; cook and stir until all of the liquid has evaporated. Add the onions; cook and stir for a couple of minutes, then pour in the sherry. Simmer for 1 minute.
3. Place half of the bread triangles into a greased baking dish with the pesto side facing up. Sprinkle half of the cheese over the bread. Spread the shrimp and crabmeat over the cheese.
4. Top with the mushroom and onion mixture, then sprinkle all but 1/2 cup of the remaining cheese over the mushrooms. Cover with the other half of the bread so that the pesto side is facing down.
5. In a large bowl, whisk together the eggs, half-and-half, salt, and cayenne pepper. Pour over the entire casserole. Cover and refrigerate for at least 2 and up to 24 hours.
6. Remove from the refrigerator for one hour before baking. Combine the 1 cup of reserved cheese with the Panko crumbs in a plastic bag.
7. Shake to blend, and sprinkle over the top of the casserole. Bake uncovered on Hi for 55 to 60 minutes in the preheated oven, or until a knife inserted in the center comes out clean.
8. Let stand for 15 minutes before serving. Garnish with fresh tomato and basil or chives.

Seafood Stuffed Zucchini
Makes 8 servings
Cook Time: 50 Min

Ingredients
4 zucchini, halved lengthwise
1 egg, beaten
1/2 pound cooked crabmeat, diced
1/2 pound cooked salad shrimp
2 teaspoons finely chopped garlic
2 tablespoons fresh lime juice
2 tablespoons fresh lemon juice
1 cup Italian seasoned bread crumbs
1 1/2 teaspoons dried oregano
1 1/2 teaspoons dried basil
1 teaspoon ground black pepper
1 cup shredded Monterey Jack cheese

Directions
1. With a large spoon, scoop out the centers of each zucchini half, reserving the meat.
2. In a large bowl, mix about 1/2 the reserved zucchini meat, the egg, crabmeat, shrimp, and garlic.
3. Blend lime juice and lemon juice into the mixture, and stir in the Italian seasoned bread crumbs. Season with oregano, basil, and pepper.
4. Arrange the zucchini halves in a medium baking dish. Generously stuff the halves with the crabmeat and shrimp mixture.
5. Bake on Hi for 35 to 45 minutes in the preheated oven, until golden brown. Remove from heat, cool slightly, and top with cheese. Return to the oven, and broil 5 minutes, or until the cheese is melted.

Seafood Stuffing
Makes 8 servings
Cook Time: 30 Min

Ingredients
1/2 cup margarine
1/2 cup chopped green bell pepper
1/2 cup chopped onion
1/2 cup chopped celery
1 pound crabmeat, drained and flaked
1/2 pound medium shrimp - peeled and deveined
1/2 cup seasoned dry bread crumbs
1 (6 ounce) package corn bread stuffing mix
2 tablespoons white sugar, divided
1 (10.75 ounce) can condensed cream of mushroom soup
1 (14.5 ounce) can chicken broth

Directions
1. Melt the margarine in a large skillet over medium heat. Add the bell pepper, onion, celery crabmeat and shrimp; cook and stir for about 5 minutes. Set aside. In a large bowl, stir together the stuffing, bread crumbs and 1 tablespoon of sugar.
2. Mix in the vegetables and seafood from the skillet. Stir in the cream of mushroom soup and as much of the chicken broth as you like. Spoon into a baking dish.
3. Bake on Hi for 30 minutes in the preheated oven, or until lightly toasted on top.

Seafood Triangles
Makes 16 servings
Cook Time: 10 Min

Ingredients
3 tablespoons chopped green onions
3 tablespoons butter, divided
1/2 pound shrimp, peeled, deveined, and quartered
1/4 cup white wine or chicken broth
4 teaspoons cornstarch
1/3 cup 2% milk
1/2 cup grated Parmesan cheese
1 (6 ounce) can crabmeat - drained, flaked and cartilage removed
1 teaspoon sugar
1 teaspoon lemon juice
1/4 teaspoon cayenne pepper
1/8 teaspoon white pepper
22 sheets phyllo dough (14 inches x 9 inches)
1 egg white, beaten

Directions
1. In a large nonstick skillet, saute onions in 1 tablespoon butter until tender. Add shrimp and wine or broth; cook and stir over medium-high heat for 2 minutes or until shrimp turn pink. Using a slotted spoon, remove shrimp.
2. Combine cornstarch and milk until smooth; stir into the cooking juices. Bring to a boil; cook and stir for 2 minutes or until thickened. Reduce heat to low. Stir in the Parmesan cheese, crab, sugar, lemon juice, cayenne, white pepper if desired and shrimp. Remove from the heat; cool.
3. On a dry surface, carefully remove two sheets of phyllo dough and place on top of each other (keep remaining dough covered with plastic wrap to prevent drying). Melt remaining butter. Cut sheets widthwise into six strips about 2 in. wide. Lightly brush the tops with butter.
4. Place a rounded teaspoonful of shrimp mixture near lower right corner of each strip. Fold left corner of dough over filling, forming a triangle. Fold

triangle up, then fold over, forming another triangle. Continue folding like a flag for the length of the strip.

5. Place triangles on ungreased baking sheets. Brush tops with egg white. Bake on Hi for 7-10 minutes or until golden brown. Serve warm.

Shrimp and Grits
Makes 8 servings
Cook Time: 1 Hr

Ingredients
4 cups chicken broth
1 teaspoon salt
1 cup quick-cooking grits
2 tablespoons margarine
1 bunch green onions, chopped
1 green bell pepper, diced
2 cloves garlic, minced
1 pound peeled and deveined small shrimp
1 cup shredded Monterey Jack cheese
3/4 cup shredded sharp Cheddar cheese
1 (10 ounce) can diced tomatoes and green chilies
1/2 teaspoon black pepper
1/4 cup shredded sharp Cheddar cheese

Directions
1. Grease a 9x12 inch baking dish.
2. Bring chicken broth and salt to a boil in a large saucepan over high heat. Stir in the grits, return to a simmer, then reduce heat to medium-low, and continue cooking for 20 minutes, stirring frequently.
3. Meanwhile, melt the margarine in a skillet over medium heat. Stir in the green onions, green pepper, and garlic; cook until the peppers have softened, about 5 minutes. Stir in the shrimp, and cook until they begin to firm.
4. Stir the Monterey Jack cheese, 3/4 cup Cheddar cheese, shrimp and vegetable mixture, canned tomatoes, and black pepper into the grits; pour into prepared baking dish and sprinkle with remaining 1/4 cup Cheddar cheese.
5. Bake on Hi until the cheese is bubbly and beginning to brown, 30 to 45 minutes.

Shrimp Casserole
Makes 6 servings

Ingredients
2 lbs peeled medium shrimp
3 cups cooked long-grain rice
1 cup sharp cheddar cheese
1 (10 3/4 ounce) cream of mushroom soup, undiluted
1 tablespoon butter

1/2 cup green onion
2 teaspoons Worcestershire sauce
1/2 teaspoon dry mustard
1/2 teaspoon fresh ground pepper
1/4 cup milk
1 teaspoon cajun seasoning

Directions
1. Green onions, peeled cooked shrimp. green onions, Worcestershire sauce, and next four ingredients.
2. Clean shrimp and devein if needed. Combine rice, shrimp, cheese, and soup in bowl. Melt butter in a large skillet over medium to high heat, and add green onions; cook, stirring constantly, until tender.
3. Stir in green onions, Worcestershire sauce, and next four ingredients. Place all mixture in a greased 10 inch round pan or 8x8 square. (The pan has to be able to fit into our oven.). Place on 1 inch rack and bake 26-28 minutes.

Shrimp Scampi
Makes 6 servings

Ingredients
4 lbs shrimp
3 Tbsp extra virgin olive oil
2 Tbsp dry white wine
8 Tbsp butter (1 stick) at room temperature
4 tsp minced garlic
1/4 cup minced shallots (or onions)
3 Tbsp minced fresh Italian parsley
1 tsp minced fresh rosemary
1 tsp grated lemon zest
2 Tbsp fresh lemon juice
1 extra-large egg yolk
2/3 cup panko (japanese bread crumbs)
Lemon wedges for serving
Kosher salt and fresh pepper to taste
1/4 tsp crushed red pepper flakes (optional...leave out if you have kids with sensitive taste buds)

Directions
1. Peel, devein, and butterfly the shrimp, leaving the tails on if you like. Place shrimp in a mixing bowl and toss gently with olive oil, wine, 2 tsp salt, and 1 tsp pepper.
2. Set aside. In a small bowl, mash the butter and garlic, shallots, parsley, rosemary, red pepper flakes, lemon zest, lemon juice, egg yolk, panko, 1/2 tsp salt, and 1/4 tsp pepper until well mixed. In a shallow, oven proof serving dish, arrange the shrimp in a single layer butterflied side own with tails curling up and toward the center of the dish.

3. Pour the remaining marinade over shrimp. Spread the butter mixture evenly over the shrimp. It's a little tricky to spread it evenly, just do your best as it will melt and disperse when baked.
4. Bake on Hi for 5-6 minutes on high until hot and bubbly. Serve with the lemon wedges.

Shrimp Scampi Bake
Makes 6 servings
Cook Time: 15 Min

Ingredients
1 cup butter
2 tablespoons prepared Dijon-style mustard
1 tablespoon fresh lemon juice
1 tablespoon chopped garlic
1 tablespoon chopped fresh parsley
2 pounds medium raw shrimp, shelled, deveined, with tails attached

Directions
1. In a small saucepan over medium heat, combine the butter, mustard, lemon juice, garlic, and parsley.
2. When the butter melts completely, remove from heat.
3. Arrange shrimp in a shallow baking dish. Pour the butter mixture over the shrimp.
4. Bake on Hi for 12 to 15 minutes or until the shrimp are pink and opaque.

Spicy Seafood Shell Appetizers
Makes 18 servings
Cook Time: 10 Min

Ingredients
1 1/2 cups mayonnaise
2/3 cup grated Parmesan cheese
2/3 cup shredded Swiss cheese
1/3 cup chopped onion
2 teaspoons Worcestershire sauce
10 drops hot pepper sauce
1 (4 ounce) can small shrimp, drained
1 (6 ounce) can crabmeat, drained and flaked
2 (2.1 ounce) packages mini phyllo tart shells
paprika

Directions
1. Lightly grease a medium baking sheet.
2. In a medium bowl, mix together mayonnaise, Parmesan cheese, Swiss cheese, onion, Worcestershire sauce and hot pepper sauce. Gently stir in shrimp and crabmeat.
3. Form phyllo dough into shells. Fill shells with the mixture.

4. Arrange stuffed shells on baking sheet. Bake on Hi for 7 to 10 minutes, or until lightly browned. Sprinkle with paprika before serving.

Swordfish a la Siciliana
Makes 6 servings
Cook Time: 20 Min

Ingredients
3 ounces raisins
5 tablespoons olive oil
1 small onion, minced
1 clove garlic, minced
1/2 pound ripe tomatoes, diced
10 green olives, pitted and minced
2 ounces pine nuts
1/4 cup capers
2 pounds swordfish steaks
salt and pepper to taste

Directions
1. Soak raisins in lukewarm water for 30 minutes. Drain and set aside.
2. Heat olive oil in a large saucepan or skillet over high heat. Saute onion and garlic until soft. Stir in raisins, tomatoes, olives, pine nuts and capers. Cover pan, reduce heat to medium and cook for 15 minutes.
3. Season the steaks with salt and pepper. Place in a lightly oiled baking dish and cover with the cooked sauce. Bake on Hi for 15 to 20 minutes, until steaks are firm.

Tuna Noodle Casserole

Makes 4 servings
Cook Time: 25 Min

Ingredients

3 cups uncooked egg noodles
1 cup chopped celery
1/3 cup chopped onion
1/4 cup chopped green pepper
1 tablespoon vegetable oil
1 (10.75 ounce) can condensed cream of
mushroom soup, undiluted
1 cup shredded Cheddar cheese
1 cup milk
1 (12 ounce) can tuna, drained and flaked
1/2 cup mayonnaise
1 (2 ounce) jar diced pimientos, drained
1/2 teaspoon salt

Directions

1. Cook noodles according to package directions.
Meanwhile, in a skillet, saute the celery, onion and
green pepper in oil until tender; set aside. In a
saucepan, combine the soup, cheese and milk.
Cook and stir over low heat until cheese is melted.
2. Drain noodles; place in a large bowl. Add the
celery mixture, soup mixture, tuna, mayonnaise,
pimientos and salt. Pour into a greased square
baking dish. Bake, uncovered, on Hi for 25-30
minutes or until heated through.

Vegetables

Asparagus Spirals
Makes 30 servings

Ingredients
1 package (17.3 ounces) Puff Pastry Sheets, thawed
6 tablespoons garlic & herb spreadable cheese, softened
8 slices prosciutto or thinly sliced deli ham
30 medium asparagus spears, trimmed

Directions
1. Unfold the pastry sheets on a lightly floured surface. Spread 3 tablespoons cheese on each pastry sheet.
2. Top each with 4 slices prosciutto. Cut each into 15 strips crosswise, making 30 in all. Tightly wrap 1 pastry strip around each asparagus spear, prosciutto-side in.
3. Place the pastries seam-side down onto baking sheets. Bake on Hi for 15 minutes or until the pastries are golden brown.

Baked Potatoes
Makes 4 servings

Ingredients
4 Medium Potatoes
Teaspoon or Table spoon of Olive Oil
Salt
Pepper

Directions
1. Cut up the potatoes. Oil a baking dish with olive oil. Place the cut up potatoes on a baking dish Sprinkle salt & pepper to your liking.
2. Bake for approximately 30 minutes on Hi.

Baked Vegetables
Makes 12 servings
Cook Time: 40 Min

Ingredients
2 medium potatoes, cut into 1/2 inch cubes
2 medium carrots, cut into 1/4 inch thick slices
1 cup fresh-cut green beans
2 medium onions, chopped
2 garlic cloves, minced
2 tablespoons olive oil or canola oil
4 medium tomatoes, chopped
2 cups cauliflowerets
1 celery rib, thinly sliced
1 teaspoon salt
1/2 teaspoon dried thyme
1/4 teaspoon dried marjoram
1/8 teaspoon pepper
1 medium zucchini, cut into 1/4-inch slices
1 medium green pepper, chopped

Directions
1. In a large saucepan, bring 1 in. of water to a boil. Add the potatoes, carrots and beans. Return to a boil. Reduce heat; cover and simmer for 10 minutes. Drain; place in a greased baking dish.
2. In a skillet, saute onions and garlic in oil until tender. Add tomatoes, cauliflower, celery and seasonings. Bring to a boil. Reduce heat; cover and simmer for 5 minutes. Spoon half over the potato mixture.
3. Top with zucchini, green pepper and remaining tomato mixture. Cover and bake on Hi for 40-45 minutes or until vegetables are tender. Serve with a slotted spoon.

Cheese and Veggie Pizza
Makes 4 servings

Ingredients
12 ounces Refrigerated Crescent Dinner Rolls
3/4 cup mayonnaise
1 teaspoon onion powder
1 teaspoon dill weed
1/2 teaspoon garlic powder
1/2 cup cheese, grated
1/4 olive, sliced

Directions
1. Press crescent rolls together to fill the bottom of the liner pan. Cook for 8-10 minutes until golden brown. Let cool.
2. Mix the rest of the ingredients and spread on cooled crust. Sprinkle finely cut vegetables on top: Broccoli, Cauliflower, carrots, fresh mushrooms, green peppers or any other vegetables you like. Cut into small squares and serve.

Cheesy Vegetable Medley
Makes 14 servings
Cook Time: 30 Min

Ingredients
3 cups broccoli florets
3 cups cauliflowerets
2 cups julienned carrots
1 small onion, diced
1/2 teaspoon garlic powder
1/2 teaspoon Italian seasoning
1/8 teaspoon salt
1/8 teaspoon pepper
8 ounces elbow macaroni, cooked and drained
2 cups shredded mozzarella cheese
2 cups shredded Cheddar cheese
8 ounces processed cheese food (eg. Velveeta), sliced
3/4 cup half-and-half cream
3/4 cup seasoned bread crumbs
1/4 cup butter or margarine
1/2 cup grated Parmesan cheese

Directions
1. Place broccoli and cauliflower in a steamer basket. Place in a saucepan over 1 in. of water; bring to a boil. Cover and steam for 5-8 minutes or until crisp-tender. Rinse in cold water; drain and set aside. Repeat with carrots and onion, steaming for 4-5 minutes or until tender.
2. Place vegetables in a bowl; add garlic powder, Italian seasoning, salt and pepper. Stir in macaroni. Spoon half into a greased baking dish. Sprinkle with half of the mozzarella, cheddar and process cheese. Repeat layers.
3. Pour cream over the top. Sprinkle with bread crumbs; dot with butter. Top with Parmesan cheese. Bake, uncovered, on Hi for 30-40 minutes or until bubbly.

Colorful Vegetable Bake
Makes 12 servings
Cook Time: 55 Min

Ingredients
3 cups frozen cut green beans, thawed and drained
2 medium green peppers, chopped
6 plum tomatoes, seeded and chopped
2 cups shredded Cheddar cheese
3 cups chopped zucchini
1 cup biscuit/baking mix
1/2 teaspoon salt
1/2 teaspoon cayenne pepper
6 eggs
1 cup milk

Directions
1. Place beans and peppers in a greased baking dish. Top with tomatoes, cheese and zucchini. In a bowl, combine the biscuit mix, salt, cayenne, eggs and milk just until moistened. Pour over the vegetables.
2. Bake, uncovered, on Hi for 55-60 minutes or until puffed and a knife inserted near the center comes out clean. Let stand for 10 minutes before serving.

Flatbread Pizza
Makes 2 servings

Ingredients
2 (6 inch) whole wheat pita bread, cut horizontally in half or 1 soft armenian lavash bread, 24x9-inch, halved
crosswise
1 (6 1/2 ounce) jar marinated artichoke hearts, drained, marinade reserved, large pieces halved
1 (6 1/2 ounce) jar marinated artichoke hearts, drained, marinade reserved, large pieces halved
1 (5 ounce) containerfeta cheese with dried basil and tomato or 1 1/2 cups crumbled flavored feta cheese
1 (14 1/2 ounce) can Italian-style diced tomatoes, drained well
1 cup pitted kalamata olives or 1 cup other brine-cured black olives, coarsely chopped
2 teaspoons dried oregano

Directions
1. Place breads on 4" rack. Brush breads with some of artichoke marinade. On HI, bake until just beginning to color, about 3 minutes.
2. Cool 5 minutes. Spread breads almost to edges with feta spread or sprinkle with crumbled feta cheese.
3. Top with tomatoes, olives, oregano and artichokes. Drizzle with remaining artichoke marinade.
4. On level HI, bake pizzas until heated through, about 4 minutes. 9 Cut into wedges.

Four-Vegetable Bake
Makes 8 servings
Cook Time: 20 Min

Ingredients
3 medium zucchini, cut into 1/4-inch slices
1 pound fresh mushrooms, sliced
1 medium onion, chopped
1/2 cup chopped green onions
8 tablespoons butter, divided
1/4 cup all-purpose flour
1 cup milk
1 (14 ounce) can water packed artichoke hearts, drained and quartered
3/4 cup shredded Swiss cheese
1/2 teaspoon salt
1/4 teaspoon pepper
3/4 cup seasoned bread crumbs

Directions
1. In a large skillet, saute the zucchini, mushrooms and onions in 3 tablespoons butter until zucchini is crisp-tender; remove and set aside. In the same skillet, melt 3 tablespoons butter. stir in flour until smooth.
2. Gradually stir in milk until blended. Bring to a boil; cook and stir for 2 minutes or until thickened. Stir in the zucchini mixture, artichokes, cheese, salt and pepper; mix well.
3. Transfer to a greased baking dish. Melt remaining butter; toss with bread crumbs. Sprinkle over the top. Bake, uncovered, on Hi for 20-25 minutes or until bubbly and topping is lightly browned.

Green Bean Casserole
Makes 10 servings

Ingredients
1 can Campbell's cream of mushroom soup.
2 cans of cut green beans
1 can of corn
1/2 cup of mushrooms (slice fresh or canned)
2 cloves of crushed garlic
6-8 slices of bacon
salt and pepper to taste
2 1/2 cups of French's Fried Onions

Directions
1. Chop the bacon into small bite size pieces, and brown in a skillet. Set aside and let cool. In a large bowl combine - green beans, corn, mushrooms, garlic, cooked bacon and cream of mushroom soup.

2. Mix completely, place in a casserole dish, and cover with French's fried onions. Bake on Hi for 25 minutes.

Herbed Vegetable Bake
Makes 6 servings
Cook Time: 20 Min

Ingredients
3 cups broccoli florets
2 cups cauliflowerets
2 medium carrots, thinly sliced
1 medium red onion, thinly sliced
1 celery rib, thinly sliced
1/2 teaspoon Italian seasoning
1/2 teaspoon dried basil
1/2 teaspoon garlic salt
2 tablespoons water
2 tablespoons reduced fat stick margarine*

Directions
1. Place the vegetables in a 9-in. square baking dish coated with nonstick cooking spray. Sprinkle with Italian seasoning, basil, garlic salt and water. Dot with margarine.
2. Cover and bake on Hi for 20-25 minutes or until vegetables are tender.

Herbed Vegetable Squares
Makes 6 servings
Cook Time: 25 Min

Ingredients
1 (10 ounce) package frozen chopped spinach, thawed and drained
2 tablespoons vegetable oil
1 1/2 cups chopped zucchini
1 (10 ounce) package frozen cut green beans, thawed
1 large onion, chopped
1/4 cup water
1 garlic clove, minced
1 1/2 teaspoons dried basil
1 1/2 teaspoons salt
1/8 teaspoon pepper
1/8 teaspoon ground nutmeg
4 eggs
1/4 cup grated Parmesan cheese
Paprika

Directions
1. Squeeze spinach dry. In a skillet, saute spinach in oil for 2 minutes. Stir in zucchini, beans, onion, water, garlic, basil, salt, pepper and nutmeg.
2. Cover and simmer for 10 minutes, stirring occasionally. Remove from the heat. In a bowl, beat eggs; gradually stir in 1-1/2 cups vegetable mixture.
3. Return all to pan and mix well. Transfer to a greased baking dish. Place in a larger baking dish; fill the larger dish with hot water to a depth of 1 in.
4. Bake on Hi for 25-30 minutes or until a knife inserted near the center comes out clean. Sprinkle with the Parmesan cheese and paprika. Let stand 10 minutes before cutting.

Mini Roasted Capsicum Tartlets
Makes 8 servings

Ingredients
2 sheets frozen ready-rolled puff pastry, partially thawed
2 x 200g tubs roasted capsicum dip
10 slices (75g) chargrilled marinated capsicum, roughly chopped
1/2 cup small fresh basil leaves

Directions
1. Lightly grease two 12-hole, 1 1/2 tablespoon-capacity round-based patty pans. Using a 6.5cm cutter, cut 12 rounds from each pastry sheet.

2. Line holes of prepared pan with pastry. Spoon 2 teaspoons of dip into each pastry case. Top with capsicum.
3. Bake on Hi for 15 minutes or until pastry is golden. Cool for 2 minutes. Top with basil. Serve.

Mixed Vegetable Bake
Makes 4 servings

Ingredients
2 cups frozen mixed vegetables, thawed
1 (8 ounce) can sliced water chestnuts, drained and halved
1 celery rib, chopped
1/4 cup chopped onion
1/2 cup mayonnaise*
1 cup shredded Cheddar cheese
1/2 cup crushed butter-flavored crackers
1 tablespoon butter or margarine, melted

Directions
1. In a bowl, combine the mixed vegetables, water chestnuts, celery, onion and mayonnaise. Stir in cheese.
2. Transfer to a greased shallow baking dish. Toss cracker crumbs and butter; sprinkle over vegetables.
3. Bake, uncovered, on Hi for 30-35 minutes or until golden brown.

Oven Fried Potatoes
Makes 5 servings

Ingredients
6-7 Baking potatoes
3-4 tablespoons olive oil
Juice of ½ lemon
Small bunch of fresh basil . chopped
3 cloves of garlic . crushed and chopped
Few dashes of red pepper flakes
Few dashes of paprika
Few dashes of black pepper

Directions
1. Wash and peel the potatoes. Pat the potatos dry and slice about ¼ inch thick. Prepare all of the ingredients for the potatoes and mix well.
2. Pour the dressing over the potatoes and toss the potatoes so the mixture is evenly distributed. Bake the potatoes on Hi or until golden.

Oven Roasted Garlic
Makes 4 servings

Ingredients
4 each Medium Garlic Heads
2 oz. Olive Oil
12 oz. Water

Directions
1. Using a sharp knife, remove the top of the garlic head to expose the inner cloves. Brush heads with olive oil and place in a shallow casserole or au gratin dish.
2. Fill dish with 1" of water and cover. Bake on Hi until garlic is soft and light brown. Check garlic for softness since oven temperatures may vary.

Oven Roasted Peppers
Makes 2 servings

Ingredients
2 or 3 medium-to-large fresh sweet bell peppers
Vegetable oil

Directions
1. Wash, core and halve peppers Remove pepper seeds and pith Arrange pepper halves in shallow baking pan skin side up, quartering pepper(s) if necessary to fit one layer in pan Lightly brush or spray oil on skin side of pepper halves, for easier pepper skin removal after roasting.
2. Place baking pan on 4. Rack Cook on High power 15 minutes (Pepper skins should blister and blacken in spots)
3. Remove NuWave cover; use tongs to rearrange peppers skin side up in pan as necessary to ensure even roasting Re-cover and cook on High power additional 10 minutes or until pepper skins are fairly evenly roasted Leave peppers in pan in covered NuWave Oven about 30 minutes or until cool enough to handle
4. This step steams the peppers, completing the cooking process. Alternatively, using tongs immediately transfer roasted peppers to bowl and cover bowl with plastic wrap until cool enough to handle.
5. Lay peppers on cutting board and slip off skins, scraping off any remaining skin with paring knife (Pepper skins remove easier while still warm, rather than chilled) Leave peppers halved, quartered or slice in strips to use as desired.

Pesto Vegetable Tart
Makes 4 servings
Cook Time: 50 Min

Ingredients
1/2 (17.3 ounce) package Pepperidge Farm® Puff Pastry Sheets
1 egg
1 tablespoon water
3 tablespoons olive oil
2 teaspoons chopped garlic
1 baby eggplant , cut diagonally in 1/2-inch thick slices
1 large zucchini , cut diagonally in 1/2-inch thick slices
1 large yellow squash , cut diagonally in 1/2-inch thick slices
1 tablespoon prepared pesto sauce
4 ounces goat cheese, crumbled
1 whole roasted sweet pepper , drained and cut into thin strips

Directions
1. Thaw the pastry sheet at room temperature for 40 minutes or until it's easy to handle. Lightly grease or line a baking sheet with parchment paper. Stir the egg and water with a fork in a small bowl.
2. Unfold the pastry sheet on a lightly floured surface. Roll the sheet into a rectangle. Place on the prepared sheet. Brush the edges of the rectangle with the egg mixture. Fold over the edges 1/2 inch on all sides, pressing firmly with a fork to form a rim. Prick the pastry thoroughly with a fork. Refrigerate for 30 minutes.
3. Stir the oil and garlic in a small bowl. Place the eggplant, zucchini and squash in a single layer on a shallow-sided pan. Brush with the oil mixture. Turn vegetables over and brush with more oil. Season to taste. Bakethe vegetables 4 minutes, turning halfway through cooking. Cool slightly.
4. Spread the pesto on the pastry. Arrange the vegetables alternately in rows. Sprinkle with the cheese.
5. Bake on Hi for 20 minutes or until golden. Sprinkle with the red pepper. Serve immediately.

Pita Chips
Makes 16 servings

Ingredients
1 Pita
Melted Butter or Olive Oil
Seasoning of your choice
I used a bit of grated Parmesan
Sesame Seeds
Salt and Pepper

Directions
1. Split each pita bread in half crosswise into two rounds. Brush the inside of each round with enough butter or oil to fully cover and sprinkle with seasoning.
2. Cut each round into 8 equal wedges, and place, seasoned side up, in a single layer on baking sheet. Prepare the chips in batches.
3. Bake on Hi until crisp and golden brown. Remove from oven and let cool slightly. Serve warm, or let cool completely and store in an airtight container.

Ratatouille
Makes 4 servings
Cook Time: 30 Min

Ingredients
1 medium eggplant, chopped
2 small zucchini, diced
6 ounces mushrooms, cut in quarters
2 tablespoons olive oil
1 (24 ounce) jar Prego® Veggie Smart Chunky & Savory Italian Sauce
1/2 teaspoon dried oregano leaves, crushed
2 tablespoons chopped fresh parsley
1 tablespoon grated Parmesan cheese

Directions
1. Place the eggplant, zucchini and mushrooms onto a rimmed baking sheet. Add the olive oil and toss to coat.
2. Roast on Hi for 25 minutes or until the vegetables are lightly browned, stirring occasionally. Remove the baking sheet from nuwave oven. Pour the sauce over the vegetables and stir to coat. Sprinkle with the oregano.
3. Roast for 5 minutes more. Sprinkle with the parsley. Serve with the cheese.

Roasted Root Vegetables
Makes 6 servings
Cook Time: 45 Min

Ingredients
1 cup diced, raw beet
4 carrots, diced
1 onion, diced
2 cups diced potatoes
4 cloves garlic, minced
1/4 cup canned garbanzo beans (chickpeas), drained
2 tablespoons olive oil
1 tablespoon dried thyme leaves
salt and pepper to taste
1/3 cup dry white wine
1 cup torn beet greens

Directions
1. Place the beet, carrot, onion, potatoes, garlic, and garbanzo beans into a baking dish.
2. Drizzle with the olive oil, then season with thyme, salt, and pepper. Mix well.
3. Bake, uncovered, on Hi for 30 minutes, stirring once midway through baking. Remove the baking dish from the oven, and stir in the wine.
4. Return to the oven, and bake until the wine has mostly evaporated and the vegetables are tender, about 15 minutes more.
5. Stir in the beet greens, allowing them to wilt from the heat of the vegetables. Season to taste with salt and pepper before serving.

Roasted Vegetable and Cornbread Stuffing
Makes 16 servings

Ingredients
1 butternut squash, peeled, seeded and diced
2 medium sweet onions, chopped
4 cloves garlic, coarsely chopped
2 teaspoons ground cumin
2 tablespoons olive oil
1/2 cup chopped fresh cilantro leaves
2 stalks celery, diced
3 cups Chicken Broth (Regular, Natural Goodness. or Certified Organic)
1 (14 ounce) package Cornbread Stuffing
1 (4 ounce) package chorizo sausage, chopped

Directions
1. Place the squash, onions and garlic into a large bowl. Add the cumin and oil and toss to coat. Spoon the squash mixture onto 2 rimmed baking sheets.
2. Roast on Hi for 30 minutes or until the squash mixture is lightly browned, stirring occasionally.
3. Reduce the temperature on or two levels. Stir the squash mixture, cilantro, celery and broth in a large bowl. Add the stuffing and mix lightly.
4. Stir in the sausage, if desired. Spoon the stuffing mixture into a greased 3 1/2-quart casserole. Cover the casserole.
5. Bake on Hi for 30 minutes or until the stuffing mixture is hot.

Roasted Vegetable Lasagna
Makes 9 servings
Cook Time: 45 Min

Ingredients
1 pound eggplant, sliced into 1/4 inch rounds
1/2 pound medium fresh mushrooms, cut into 1/4 inch slices
3 small zucchini, cut lengthwise into 1/4-inch slices
2 sweet red pepper, cut lenthwise into 6 pieces each
3 tablespoons olive oil
1 clove garlic, minced
1 teaspoon salt
1/2 teaspoon pepper
1 (15 ounce) container reduced-fat ricotta cheese
1/4 cup grated Parmesan cheese
1/4 cup egg substitute
1 (26 ounce) jar meatless spaghetti sauce
12 no-boil lasagna noodles
2 cups shredded part-skim mozzarella cheese
3 tablespoons minced fresh basil

Directions
1. Coat two baking pans with nonstick cooking spray. Place eggplant and mushrooms on a prepared pan.
2. Place the zucchini and red pepper on the second pan. Combine the oil and garlic; brush over both sides of vegetables. Sprinkle with salt and pepper.
3. Bake, uncovered, on Hi for 15 minutes. Turn vegetables over. Bake 15 minutes longer. Remove eggplant and mushrooms.
3. Bake zucchini and red pepper 5-10 minutes longer or until edges are browned.
4. In a bowl, combine the ricotta cheese, Parmesan cheese and egg substitute. Spread about 1/4 cup pasta sauce in a baking dish coated with nonstick cooking spray.
5. Layer with four lasagna noodles (noodleswill overlap slightly), half of ricotta cheese mixture, half of vegetables, a third of pasta sauce and 2/3 cup mozzarella cheese. Sprinkle with half of basil. Repeat layers.
6. Top with the remaining noodles and pasta sauce. Cover and bake on Hi for 40 minutes. Uncover; sprinkle with remaining cheese.
7. Bake 5-10 minutes longer or until edges are bubbly and cheese is melted. Let stand for 10 minutes before cutting.

Roasted Vegetable Medley
Makes 6 servings

Ingredients
2 tablespoons olive oil, divided
1 large yam, peeled and cut into 1 inch pieces
1 large parsnip, peeled and cut into 1 inch pieces
1 cup baby carrots
1 zucchini, cut into 1 inch slices
1 bunch fresh asparagus, trimmed and cut into 1 inch pieces
1/2 cup roasted red peppers, cut into 1-inch pieces
2 cloves garlic, minced
1/4 cup chopped fresh basil
1/2 teaspoon kosher salt
1/2 teaspoon ground black pepper

Directions
1. Grease 2 baking sheets with 1 tablespoon olive oil.
2. Place the yams, parsnips, and carrots onto the baking sheets. Bake on Hi for 30 minutes, then add the zucchini and asparagus, and drizzle with the remaining 1 tablespoon of olive oil. Continue baking until all of the vegetables are tender, about 30 minutes more.
3. Once tender, remove from the nuwave oven, and allow to cool for 30 minutes on the baking sheet.
4. Toss the roasted peppers together with the garlic, basil, salt, and pepper in a large bowl until combined. Add the roasted vegetables, and toss to mix. Serve at room temperature or cold.

Root Vegetable Gratin
Makes 6 servings
Cook Time: 1 Hr 20 Min

Ingredients
3 tablespoons unsalted butter, softened
1 (1 1/2) pound butternut squash, peeled and thinly sliced
1 pound red potatoes, peeled and thinly sliced*
1 pound bulb celery root (celeriac), peeled, cut in half and thinly sliced
1 bunch leek, washed well, white and green part only, thinly sliced
1 3/4 cups Swanson® Vegetable Broth (regular or Certified Organic)
1/2 cup heavy cream
1 teaspoon minced fresh thyme leaves
1/2 teaspoon ground nutmeg
1/3 cup grated Parmesan cheese

Directions
1. Spread the butter in a baking dish. Add the squash, potatoes, celery root and leeks into the prepared dish.
2. Heat the broth, cream, thyme and nutmeg in a 2-quart saucepan over medium heat to a boil. Season to taste.
3. Pour the broth mixture over the vegetables and toss to coat.
4. Bake on Hi for 25 minutes. Reduce the by 1 or 2 levels and bake for 40 minutes more, or until golden brown and the vegetables are tender. (If the vegetables are browning too fast in the first 25 minutes, cover the dish loosely with foil.)
5. Sprinkle with the cheese. Let stand for 10 minutes.

Spinach Calzones with Homemade Marinara Sauce
Makes 4 servings

Ingredients
2 prepared pizza doughs
2 packages of spinach (10 ounces each)
1 medium-large onion, finely chopped
5 cloves of garlic, finely chopped
1 cup ricotta cheese
½ cup parmesan cheese, grated
½ cup mozzarella, shredded
About 8-10 slices of deli ham, cut into long strips
Salt & Pepper to taste
Approximately 4 tablespoons Olive Oil
Dashes of Living the Gourmet Dry Herb Rub
29 oz. can of crushed tomatoes
5 cloves of garlic . chopped
1 yellow onion . sliced
Healthy handful of fresh basil
Dashes of fresh ground black pepper
Pinch of sugar
Dashes of sea salt
Dashes of oregano
Drizzles of Olive Oil

Directions
1. In an large skillet on medium low heat, drizzle about 2 tablespoons of olive oil. Add onion and sauté until tender and golden. Then add garlic and spinach, sautéing until large clumps are broken up.
2. Add the dashes of salt and pepper. Transfer to a medium bowl and let cool. Once cool enough, stir in ricotta, parmesan, mozzarella, and ham.
3. Prepare 2 baking sheets by lining them with parchment paper and sprinkling the paper with cornmeal. Set aside.
4. Flour the pizza dough and work the dough using your fists into a large circle, do not roll the dough out, about 12 inch circles. Fill one half side with spinach mixture and fold over.
5. Press the edges with a fork to seal the calzone. Transfer the dough onto the cookie sheets. Rub each calzone with a tablespoon of olive oil and bake on Hi for 25 minutes or until golden.
6. Heat a large frying pan with a drizzle of olive oil and add the basil, garlic and sliced onions. Heat until the onion is clear.
7. Add the crushed tomato and the spices and the pinch of sugar. Simmer on low for about 25-30 minutes.

Spinach Rolls
Makes 4 servings

Ingredients
8 lasagna noodles, cooked and drained sauce
1 medium onion, finely chopped
2 garlic cloves, minced
1 tablespoon butter
3 cups tomato sauce
1 teaspoon oregano
1/2 teaspoon thyme leaves
1/2 teaspoon basil
1/4 cup chopped mushroom (optional)
1 (10 ounce) package frozen chopped spinach
1 cup ricotta cheese
2 tablespoons parmesan cheese
1 egg
1 dash pepper

Directions
1. Saute onion and garlic in butter until vegetables are tender. Add tomato sauce, seasonings and mushrooms. Simmer (sauce).
2. Cook spinach according to package directions. Drain and squeeze out excess water. Blend together spinach, cheeses, pepper and egg.
3. Spread the mixture evenly along the entire length of each noodle. Lay sausage on top of cheese mixture.
4. Roll each one and place on its side in the liner pan which has been lightly greased. Cover with sauce. Bake in the NuWave on power level HI for 15 minutes or until heated through.

Steak Fries
Makes 5 servings

Ingredients
Number of servings
8-10 potatoes . cleaned with skin
1 ½ tablespoons of Living the Gourmet Signature Spice Rub
4 tablespoons olive oil

Directions
1. Clean and slice the potatoes and pat them dry with a paper towel. Place the potato slices in a large bowl.
2. Add the Living the Gourmet Signature Spice Rub and the olive oil and toss well so that each potato is coated with the spices.
3. Place potatoes in a baking dish and place in the Nuwave. Cook on Hi for 20 min then loosen the potatoes carefully with a spatula and turn them over. Bake again until golden brown.

Stuffed Baked Onions
Makes 8 servings
Cook Time: 45 Min

Ingredients
8 medium onion, peeled
4 bacon strips, diced
3/4 cup finely chopped carrots
1/2 cup finely chopped sweet red pepper
1 1/2 cups soft bread crumbs
1/3 cup minced fresh parsley
3 tablespoons butter, melted
1 1/2 teaspoons salt
1/2 teaspoon pepper
3/4 cup beef broth

Directions
1. Cut 1/2 in. off the top of each onion; trim bottom so onion sits flat. Scoop out center, leaving a 1/2-in. shell. Chop remaining onion, set 1/2 cup aside (discarding remaining onion or save for another use). Place onion shells in a Dutch oven or large saucepan and cover with water. Bring to a boil; reduce heat and cook for 8-10 minutes.
2. Meanwhile, in a large skillet, cook bacon over medium heat until crisp. Remove to paper towels; drain, reserving 1 teaspoon drippings. In same skillet, saute the chopped onion, carrots and red pepper in dripping for 8 minutes or until tender.
3. Remove from the heat; stir in the bread crumbs, parsley, butter, salt, pepper and bacon. Drain onion shells; fill each with about 1/3 cup vegetable mixture. Place in an ungreased shallow baking dish. Pour broth over onions.
4. Cover and bake on Hi for 45-50 minutes or until heated through.

Sweet Onion Dip
Makes 6 servings

Ingredients
2 large chopped onions, medium dice
2 cups parmesan cheese
2 cups low-fat mayonnaise
1/2 teaspoon black pepper

Directions
1. Mix all ingredients in a 10inch baking pan. Smooth the ingredients flat and place on the 1inch rack.
2. On power level HI, cook for 15 minutes or until it turns brown and bubbly. Serve with your favorite cracker or bread.

Sweet Potato Souffle
Makes 6 servings

Ingredients
4 cups mashed sweet potatoes
1 cup sugar
2 eggs
1/2 cup milk
1/2 teaspoon salt
1/4 cup butter (melted)
1 teaspoon vanilla
1 cup brown sugar
1/2 cup flour
1/3 cup butter (melted)
1 cup pecans

Directions
1. Mix together sweet potatoes, sugar, eggs, milk, salt and 2 1/3 stick of melted butter. Pour into a buttered pan.
2. Mix together all topping ingredients and crumble topping evenly over potato mixture. Place pan on 1" rack and cook for 25-30 minutes uncovered.

Swiss Vegetable Medley
Makes 6 servings
Cook Time: 35 Min

Ingredients
1 (16 ounce) package frozen broccoli, carrots and cauliflower, thawed and drained
1 (10.75 ounce) can condensed cream of mushroom soup, undiluted
1/2 cup sour cream
1/4 teaspoon pepper
1 (4 ounce) jar chopped pimientos, drained
1 cup shredded Swiss cheese, divided
1 (2.8 ounce) can French-fried onions, divided

Directions
1. In a bowl, combine vegetables, soup, sour cream, pepper, pimientos and 1/2 cup cheese. Stir in half of the onions; mix well.
2. Pour into an ungreased casserole dish. Cover and bake on Hi for 30-35 minutes or until bubbly.
3. Uncover; sprinkle with remaining cheese and onions. Return to the oven until cheese is melted, about 5 minutes.

Vegetable Focaccia
Makes 12 servings
Cook Time: 15 Min

Ingredients
2 cups bread flour
1 (.25 ounce) package quick-rise yeast
1 teaspoon salt
1 cup warm water (120 to 130 degrees F)
1 tablespoon olive or canola oil
3 plum tomatoes, chopped
5 medium fresh mushrooms, sliced
1/2 cup chopped green pepper
1/2 cup sliced ripe olives
1/4 cup chopped onion
3 tablespoons olive or canola oil
2 teaspoons red wine vinegar or cider vinegar
3/4 teaspoon salt
1/4 teaspoon garlic powder
1/4 teaspoon dried oregano
1/4 teaspoon pepper
2 teaspoons cornmeal

Directions
1. In a mixing bowl, combine 2 cups flour, yeast and salt. Add water and oil; beat until smooth. Stir in enough remaining flour to form a soft dough.
2. Turn onto a floured surface; knead until smooth and elastic, about 4 minutes. Cover and let rest for 15 minutes.
3. Meanwhile, in a bowl, combine the tomatoes, mushrooms, green pepper, olives, onion, oil, vinegar and seasonings.
4. Coat a baking pan with nonstick cooking spray; sprinkle with cornmeal. Press dough into pan. Prick dough generously with a fork.
5. Bake on Hi for 5 minutes or until lightly browned. Cover with vegetable mixture. Bake 8-10 minutes longer or until edges of crust are golden.

Vegetable Frittata
Makes 4 servings
Cook Time: 15 Min

Ingredients
4 slices bacon, cut into 1/2 inch pieces
2 cups frozen shredded hash browns, thawed
1 cup chopped broccoli
1/2 cup chopped green pepper
1/2 cup chopped red onion
1/2 teaspoon dried rosemary, crushed
6 eggs
3 tablespoons water
1/2 teaspoon salt
1/4 teaspoon pepper
1/4 teaspoon paprika

Directions
1. In a 8-in. skillet, cook the bacon until crisp. Drain, reserving 2 tablespoons drippings in the skillet. Remove bacon to paper towel.
2. To the skillet, add hash browns, broccoli, green pepper, onion and rosemary; cover and cook over low heat until has browns are golden brown vegetables are tender, about 10 minutes.
3. Remove from the heat and set aside. Beat eggs, water, salt and pepper; pour over hash browns. Top with bacon and paprika.
4. Bake, uncovered, on hi for 12-15 minutes or until eggs are completely set.

Vegetable Lasagna
Makes 6 servings

Ingredients
1 (12 ounce) package lasagna noodles (no cooking needed)
2 eggs, beaten
1 (16 ounce) container part-skim ricotta cheese
2 (10 3/4 ounce) cans condensed cream of mushroom soup
2 cups cheddar cheese (shredded)
1 cup parmesan cheese (grated)
1 cup sour cream
1 ounce garlic and herb seasoning (soup mix or can us onion soup mix)
1 (10 ounce) package frozen broccoli, thawed & chopped fine
1 (10 ounce) package frozen carrots (grated)

Directions
1. Grease a 9x13 inch baking dish. In a medium bowl combine eggs, ricotta cheese, mushroom soup, Cheddar cheese, Parmesan cheese, sour cream and soup mix.
2. In prepared dish layer noodles, cheese mixture, broccoli, carrots. Repeat layers with remaining ingredients, ending with cheese.
3. Place in Nuwave covered, on Hi heat for 15 minute Uncover and cook an additional 15 minutes on Hi.

Vegetable Stuffing Bake
Makes 6 servings
Cook Time: 35 Min

Ingredients
4 cups Herb Seasoned Stuffing
2 tablespoons butter, melted
1 (10.75 ounce) can Condensed Cream of
Mushroom Soup (Regular, 98% Fat Free or 25%
Less Sodium)
1/2 cup sour cream
2 small zucchini, shredded
2 medium carrots, chopped
1 small onion, finely chopped

Directions
1. Stir 1 cup of the stuffing and butter in a small
bowl. Set aside.
2. Stir soup, sour cream, zucchini, carrots and
onion in a large bowl., Add the remaining stuffing
and stir lightly to coat.
3. Spoon the mixture into a baking dish. Sprinkle
with the reserved stuffing mixture.
4. Bake on Hi for 35 minutes or until it's hot.

Zucchini and Yellow Squash Casserole
Makes 3 servings

Ingredients
All-purpose flour, for dusting
2 medium green zucchini
2 medium yellow squash
Coarse salt and freshly ground pepper
2 tablespoons unsalted butter
1 small onion, diced
1/2 cup grated Gruyere cheese (1 ounce)
1/4 cup egg substitute
1 large egg yolk
1/4 cup heavy cream
Extra-virgin olive oil, for brushing

Directions
1. Spray rectangular baking dish. Very thinly slice 1
green zucchini and 1 yellow squash lengthwise.
Place slices in a colander in a single layer, and
sprinkle lightly with salt.
2. Place colander in a bowl, and set aside to drain
for 30 minutes. Cut the remaining zucchini and
squash into 1/3-inch dice. In a large skillet, melt
butter over high heat.
3. Add onion and diced squash, and season with
salt and pepper. Cook until golden brown but still
firm, about 8 minutes.

4. Evenly distribute cooked vegetables in the pan.
Sprinkle Gruyere on top. Place salted squash slices
between double layers of paper towels.
5. Gently press down to remove as much liquid as
possible. Alternating squash colors, weave a lattice
pattern over the top of the cheese and vegetables,
covering the entire surface.
6. Trim or tuck in ends to fit. In a medium bowl,
whisk together egg substitute, egg yolk, and cream,
and season with salt and pepper. Lift the edges of
the lattice in several places, and pour in the egg
mixture.
7. Using a pastry brush, coat the lattice with olive
oil. It may be necessary to spray lattice with
cooking spray while baking if it is not browning
sufficiently.
8. Bake, loosely covered with aluminum foil on Hi
until the custard is set, 30 to 35 minutes. Place on a
wire rack to cool slightly before serving.

Zucchini and Yellow Squash Gratin

Ingredients
2 tablespoons butter
2 medium zucchini, sliced crosswise inch thick
2 medium yellow squash, sliced crosswise inch
thick
2 shallots, minced
2 garlic cloves, minced
Sea salt and ground pepper
1/2 cup greek-style yogurt or low-fat cottage
cheese
1 cup panko crumbs
1/2 cup grated Parmesan cheese

Directions
1. In a large skillet, melt butter over medium heat;
add zucchini, yellow squash, shallots, and garlic.
Season with salt and pepper.
2. Cook, stirring occasionally, until zucchini and
squash are crisp-tender, 4 to 6 minutes. Add yogurt
or cottage cheese, and cook until thickened, about
5 minutes.
3. Remove skillet from heat; stir in 1/2 cup panko
and cup Parmesan. Spoon mixture into a shallow
baking dish.
4. Sprinkle with remaining panko and Parmesan;
season with salt and pepper. Bake on Hi until top is
golden, 8 to 10 minutes.

Holiday Favorites

1-Dish Taco Bake
Makes 6 servings
Cook Time: 30 Min

Ingredients
1 pound ground beef
1 (1.25 ounce) package taco seasoning
Mazola Pure® Cooking Spray
3/4 cup all-purpose flour
1/2 cup masa corn flour OR corn meal
2 envelopes Fleischmann's® RapidRise Yeast
1 tablespoon sugar
1/2 teaspoon salt
3/4 cup very warm milk (120 degrees F to 130 degrees F)
3 tablespoons Mazola® Corn Oil
1 egg
1 cup chunky salsa
1 cup shredded Mexican-style cheese
1 cup corn chips, partially crushed

Directions
1. Brown ground beef and drain. Add taco seasoning and mix well.
2. Mix batter ingredients together in a pre-sprayed deep dish pie plate.
3. Top batter with taco meat filling. Pour salsa evenly over meat; sprinkle with shredded cheese and corn chips.
4. Bake on Hi for 30 minutes or until done.

After-Christmas Turkey Potpie
Makes 6 servings
Cook Time: 55 Min

Ingredients
1 cup sliced carrots
1 cup finely chopped onion
1/2 cup chopped celery
1/2 teaspoon dried thyme
1/8 teaspoon pepper
3 tablespoons butter or margarine
2 cups cubed cooked turkey
1 tablespoon all-purpose flour
1 (10.75 ounce) can condensed golden mushroom soup, undiluted
1 cup frozen cut green beans, cooked and drained
1 Pastry for double-crust pie (9 inches)
1 tablespoon milk

Directions
1. In a skillet, saute carrots, onion, celery, thyme and pepper in butter until vegetables are crisp-tender. In a large resealable plastic bag, combine turkey and flour; shake to coat.
2. Add turkey, soup and green beans to the vegetable mixture; mix well. Line a pie plate with bottom crust. Add turkey mixture. Roll out remaining pastry to fit top of pie; seal and flute edges.
3. Cut slits in pastry. Brush with milk. Cover edges loosely with foil. Bake on Hi for 55-65 minutes or until golden brown. Serve warm.

Apple Cranberry Crisp
Makes 6 servings
Cook Time: 30 Min

Ingredients
1 1/2 cups quick cooking oats
1/2 cup brown sugar
1/3 cup all-purpose flour
1 teaspoon ground cinnamon
1/3 cup butter flavored shortening, melted
1 tablespoon water
1 (16 ounce) can whole berry cranberry sauce
2 tablespoons cornstarch
5 Granny Smith apples - peeled, cored and thinly sliced

Directions
1. In a medium bowl, mix together the oats, brown sugar, flour, and cinnamon. Stir in the melted shortening and water to form a crumbly mixture.
2. In a large saucepan, mix together the cranberry sauce and cornstarch. Bring to a boil, and then remove from heat. Stir in the apples. Spread into a glass baking dish. Crumble the oat mixture over the apples.
3. Bake on Hi for 30 to 35 minutes, or until the apples are tender. Serve warm.

Apple Cream Coffee Cake
Makes 12 servings
Cook Time: 40 Min

Ingredients
1/2 cup chopped walnuts
2 teaspoons ground cinnamon
1 1/2 cups sugar, divided
1/2 cup butter or margarine, softened
2 eggs
1 teaspoon vanilla extract
2 cups all-purpose flour
1 teaspoon baking powder
1/2 teaspoon baking soda
1/2 teaspoon salt
1 cup sour cream
1 medium apple - peeled, cored and thinly sliced

Directions
1. Combine nuts, cinnamon and 1/2 cup sugar; set aside. In a large mixing bowl, cream butter; gradually add remaining sugar, beating until light and fluffy.
2. Add eggs, one at a time, beating well after each addition. Blend in vanilla. Combine dry ingredients; add to creamed mixture alternately with sour cream, beating well after each addition. Spread half of the batter in a well greased tube pan with a removable bottom.
3. Top with apple slices; sprinkle with half of the nut mixture. To with remaining batter, then with remaining nut mixture.
4. Bake on Hi for 40 minutes or until cake tests done. Remove from oven; let stand 30 minutes. Loosen sides of cake; lift cake with removable bottom from pan. Cool. Before serving, carefully lift cake from pan.

Apple Crisp Pie
Makes 8 servings
Cook Time: 40 Min

Ingredients
1/2 cup butter, softened
2 ounces cream cheese, softened
1 1/4 cups all-purpose flour
2 tablespoons white sugar
1/4 teaspoon salt
6 cups Granny Smith apples - peeled, cored and thinly sliced
1 tablespoon lemon juice
1/4 cup brown sugar
2 tablespoons all-purpose flour
1/2 teaspoon ground cinnamon
1/4 teaspoon ground nutmeg
1/8 teaspoon ground ginger
1/4 cup brown sugar
2 tablespoons all-purpose flour
10 tablespoons quick cooking oats
6 tablespoons butter

Directions
1. Spray a pie dish with cooking spray.
2. To make the crust, beat 1/2 cup of butter with cream cheese in a mixing bowl with an electric mixer until thoroughly combined; scrape the sides of mixing bowl occasionally to incorporate all the butter and cream cheese. Beat in 1 1/4 cups flour, the white sugar, and salt on medium-low speed until the mixture looks like coarse cornmeal, about 20 seconds. Increase the speed to medium-high, and beat until the dough begins to clump together, about 30 more seconds.
3. Lay out a 24-inch piece of waxed paper on a work surface, and scoop the dough out onto the left half of the paper. Form it into a ball, and flatten it into a 6-inch disk; fold the right side of the paper over the dough disk, covering the dough. With the rolling pin on top of the paper, gently roll the dough out into a round crust about 1/8-inch thick; peel off the top half of the waxed paper, turn the dough out onto the prepared pie dish, and fit the dough into the dish. Peel of the remaining portion of waxed paper.
4. To make the filling, mix together the apples and lemon juice in a bowl. In a small bowl, mix 1/4 cup of brown sugar, 2 tablespoons of flour, the cinnamon, nutmeg, and ginger together until thoroughly combined, then mix the flour mixture with the apples. Pour the apple filling into the crust.
5. To make the topping, combine 1/4 cup of brown sugar, 2 tablespoons of flour, and the oats; with a pastry cutter, cut in 6 tablespoons of butter, until the mixture looks like coarse crumbs. Spoon the topping evenly over the apple filling.
6. Bake on Hi until the apple filling is bubbling and the topping is golden brown, about 40 minutes. If the crust begins to look brown after about 20 minutes of baking, cover the crust edge with a strip of aluminum foil.

Apple Pie Ham
Makes 6 servings
Cook Time: 1 Hr

Ingredients
1 (4 pound) fully-cooked, bone-in ham
1 (20 ounce) can apple pie filling
1 tablespoon prepared yellow mustard
2 tablespoons barbeque sauce
2 tablespoons honey

Directions
1. Place the ham in a baking dish or roasting pan and cover tightly with aluminum foil.
2. Roast for 30 minutes on Hi. While the ham roasts, mix together the apple pie filling, mustard, barbeque sauce and honey. Coat ham with the mixture when the 30 minutes are up.
3. Return to the nuwave oven uncovered and cook for an additional 30 minutes or until ham is heated through.

Apple Turkey Potpie
Makes 6 servings
Cook Time: 25 Min

Ingredients
1/4 cup chopped onion
1 tablespoon butter or margarine
2 (10.75 ounce) cans condensed cream of chicken soup, undiluted
3 cups cubed cooked turkey
1 large unpeeled tart apples, cubed
1/3 cup golden raisins
1 teaspoon lemon juice
1/4 teaspoon ground nutmeg
1 (9 inch) pie crust

Directions
1. In a large saucepan, sauté onion in butter until tender. Add the soup, turkey, apple, raisins, lemon juice and nutmeg; mix well.
2. Spoon into an ungreased baking dish. On a lightly floured surface, roll out pastry to fit top of dish. Place over filling; flute edges and cut slits in top.
3. Bake on Hi for 25-30 minutes or until crust is golden brown and filling is bubbly.

Artichokes Au Gratin
Makes 4 servings
Cook Time: 20 Min

Ingredients
2 (14 ounce) cans water-packed artichoke hearts, drained and quartered
1 garlic clove, minced
1/4 cup butter, divided
2 tablespoons all-purpose flour
1/2 teaspoon salt
1/4 teaspoon pepper
1 1/2 cups milk
1 egg, lightly beaten
1/2 cup shredded Swiss cheese, divided
1 tablespoon dry bread crumbs
1/8 teaspoon paprika

Directions
1. In a skillet, saute the artichokes and garlic in 2 tablespoons butter until tender. Transfer to a greased baking dish.
2. In a saucepan, melt the remaining butter. Stir in flour, salt and pepper until smooth. Gradually add milk. Bring to a boil; cook and stir for 2 minutes or until thickened. Remove from the heat. Stir a small amount of hot mixture into egg; return all to pan, stirring constantly. Stir in 1/4 cup cheese until melted.
3. Pour over artichokes; sprinkle with remaining cheese. Combine crumbs and paprika; sprinkle over top. Bake, uncovered, on Hi for 20-25 minutes or until heated through.

Asparagus Quiche
Makes 12 servings
Cook Time: 35 Min

Ingredients
1 pound fresh asparagus, trimmed and cut into 1/2 inch pieces
10 slices bacon
2 (8 inch) unbaked pie shells
1 egg white, lightly beaten
4 eggs
1 1/2 cups half-and-half cream
1/4 teaspoon ground nutmeg
salt and pepper to taste
2 cups shredded Swiss cheese

Directions
1. Place asparagus in a steamer over 1 inch of boiling water, and cover. Cook until tender but still firm, about 2 to 6 minutes. Drain and cool.

2. Place bacon in a large, deep skillet. Cook over medium high heat until evenly brown. Drain, crumble and set aside.

3. Brush pie shells with beaten egg white. Sprinkle crumbled bacon and chopped asparagus into pie shells.

4. In a bowl, beat together eggs, cream, nutmeg, salt and pepper. Sprinkle Swiss cheese over bacon and asparagus. Pour egg mixture on top of cheese.

5. Bake uncovered on Hi until firm, about 35 to 40 minutes.

Autumn Squash Casserole
Makes 8 servings
Cook Time: 20 Min

Ingredients
3 pounds buttercup squash - peeled, seeded, and cut into 3/4-inch chunks
1/4 cup butter
1 tablespoon brown sugar
1/4 teaspoon salt
1 dash white pepper
1 1/2 tablespoons butter
6 cups sliced peeled apples
1/4 cup white sugar
1 1/2 cups cornflakes cereal, coarsely crushed
1/2 cup chopped pecans
1/2 cup brown sugar
2 tablespoons melted butter

Directions
1. Place the squash pieces in a saucepan and cover with water. Bring to a boil and cook until the squash is tender, about 15 minutes. Drain; then mash the squash with 1/4 cup butter, 1 tablespoon brown sugar, salt, and white pepper.

2. Heat the 1 1/2 tablespoons butter in a large skillet over low heat; stir in sliced apples and sprinkle with the white sugar. Cover and cook over low heat until barely tender, about 5 minutes, stirring occasionally. Spread the apples in a casserole dish. Spoon the mashed squash evenly over the apples.

3. Stir together the cornflakes, pecans, the 1/2 cup brown sugar, and melted butter. Sprinkle the cornflake mixture evenly over the squash. 4. Bake on Hi until heated through, about 15 minutes.

Avocado Stuffed Yams
Makes 4 servings
Cook Time: 40 Min

Ingredients
4 (8 ounce) yams

1 medium red bell pepper, seeded and diced
2 avocados - peeled, pitted, and mashed
1/4 cup chopped fresh cilantro
1/4 cup olive oil
2 green onions, sliced
1/2 teaspoon ground cumin
3 tablespoons lime juice
salt and ground black pepper to taste
1 cup shredded Cheddar cheese

Directions
1. Place yams on a baking sheet.

2. Bake yams on Hi for 40 minutes, or until tender, turning occasionally. Set aside.

3. In a medium bowl, mix together the red pepper, avocado, cilantro, olive oil, green onions, cumin and lime juice.

4. Cut yams in half lengthwise, and fluff the centers with a fork. Top with the avocado stuffing. Season with salt and pepper, and top with shredded Cheddar cheese.

Baked Apples with Sweet Potato Stuffing
Makes 6 servings

Ingredients
6 baking apples - peeled and cored
1/2 cup cinnamon red hot candies
1 cup water
1 (29 ounce) can sweet potatoes, drained
1/3 cup packed brown sugar
1/2 cup crushed pineapple, drained
1/4 cup chopped pecans
6 large marshmallows

Directions
1. In a large pot over medium heat, combine the candies and water. Stir until candies are dissolved.

2. Add the apples and baste frequently until apples begin to soften. Remove from heat and allow to cool.

3. Mix together the sweet potatoes, brown sugar, pineapple and pecans.

4. Stuff the cooled apples with the sweet potato mixture. Mound any remaining mixture on top of apples.

5. Place in a casserole dish and bake for 20 minutes on Hi; place a marshmallow on each apple, return to nuwave and cook until marshmallows are golden brown.

Baked Corn Beef Hash
Makes 4 servings
Cook Time: 30 Min

Ingredients
1 tablespoon vegetable oil
1 onion, sliced
1 (14 ounce) can baked beans
1 (12 ounce) can corned beef, chopped
2 tablespoons tomato puree
1 dash Worcestershire sauce
2 cups mashed potatoes
1 cup shredded extra-sharp Cheddar cheese

Directions
1. Heat the vegetable oil in a skillet over medium heat. Add the onion, and cook until the onion has softened and turned translucent, about 5 minutes.
2. Meanwhile, spread the baked beans in a casserole dish. Toss the corned beef with the tomato puree and Worcestershire sauce in a bowl and sprinkle over the beans.
3. Spread the onions overtop, followed by the mashed potatoes. Finally, sprinkle with the shredded Cheddar cheese. 2. Bake on Hi for 30 minutes until the casserole is hot and bubbly.

Baked Corn Pudding
Makes 10 servings
Cook Time: 45 Min

Ingredients
1/2 cup sugar
3 tablespoons all-purpose flour
3 eggs
1 cup milk
1/4 cup butter, melted
1/2 teaspoon salt
1/2 teaspoon pepper
1 (15.25 ounce) can whole kernel corn, drained
1 (14.75 ounce) can cream-style corn

Directions
1. In a bowl, combine the sugar and flour. Whisk in the eggs, milk, butter, salt and pepper. Stir in the corn and cream-style corn.
2. Pour into a greased baking dish. Bake, uncovered, on Hi for 45-50 minutes or until a knife inserted near the center comes out clean.

Baked French Toast With Maple Syrup and Granola
Makes 12 servings
Cook Time: 45 Min

Ingredients
1 (1 pound) loaf challah bread, sliced 1/2-inch thick
4 eggs
1 quart half-and-half cream
1/2 cup orange juice
1/2 cup white sugar
1/2 cup light brown sugar
1 teaspoon ground cinnamon
1/2 teaspoon ground nutmeg
1 cup granola cereal
1/2 cup maple syrup
1/2 cup unsalted butter, melted

Directions
1. Butter a baking dish. Lay the bread slices into the prepared baking dish in 2 layers. Beat eggs, half-and-half cream, orange juice, white sugar, brown sugar, cinnamon, and nutmeg together in a bowl until smooth, and pour over the bread.
2. With a large spoon, press the bread down into the egg mixture so all the bread becomes soaked with the mixture.
3. Sprinkle the granola evenly over the casserole, and drizzle with maple syrup and melted butter. Cover the dish with plastic wrap, and refrigerate overnight.
4. About 1 hour before serving, remove the casserole from the refrigerator, and take off the plastic wrap.
5. Bake on Hi for 45 minutes or until browned. Serve warm.

Baked Ham
Makes 18 servings
Cook Time: 5 Hrs

Ingredients
1 (12 pound) bone-in ham, rump portion
1/2 cup whole cloves
1 cup packed brown sugar
4 cups water, or as needed

Directions
1. Place ham in a roasting pan, and press whole cloves into the top at 1 to 2 inch intervals. Pack the top with a layer of brown sugar.
2. Pour enough water into the bottom of the roasting pan to come to a 1 inch depth. Cover the pan tightly with aluminum foil or a lid.
3. Bake on Hi for 4 to 5 hours in the about 22 minutes per pound, or until the internal temperature of the ham has reached 160 degrees.
4. Make sure the meat thermometer is not touching the bone. Let stand for about 20 minutes before carving.

Baked Ham with Maple Glaze
Makes 8 servings
Cook Time: 1 Hr 30 Min

Ingredients
1 (5 pound) fully-cooked, bone-in ham
1/4 cup maple syrup
1 tablespoon red wine vinegar
2 tablespoons Dijon mustard
1 tablespoon dry mustard

Directions
1. Trim excess fat off the ham and score in a diamond pattern with a sharp knife, making shallow cuts about 1 inch apart. Place in a roasting pan.
2. Roast on Hi for 30 minutes. In a small bowl, mix together the maple syrup, red wine vinegar, Dijon mustard and mustard powder.
3. When the 30 minutes are up, brush 1/3 of the glaze over the ham. Bake 20 minutes, and repeat twice with remaining glaze. Let the ham stand for 10 to 15 minutes before carving.

Baked Potato Pizza
Makes 8 servings
Cook Time: 15 Min

Ingredients
1 (6.5 ounce) package pizza crust mix
3 medium unpeeled potatoes, baked and cooled
1 tablespoon butter or margarine, melted
1/4 teaspoon garlic powder
1/4 teaspoon dried Italian seasoning
1 cup sour cream
6 bacon strips, cooked and crumbled
3 green onions, chopped
1 1/2 cups shredded mozzarella cheese
1/2 cup shredded Cheddar cheese

Directions
1. Prepare crust according to package directions. Press dough into a lightly greased pizza pan; build up edges slightly. Bake on Hi for 5-6 minutes or until crust is firm and begins to brown.
2. Cut potatoes into 1/2-in. cubes. In a bowl, combine butter, garlic powder and Italian seasoning.
3. Add potatoes and toss. Spread sour cream over crust; top with potato mixture, bacon, onions and cheeses.
4. Bake on Hi for 15-20 minutes or until cheese is lightly browned. Let stand for 5 minutes before cutting.

Barbecued Sticky Ribs
Makes 6 servings
Cook Time: 1 Hr 20 Min

Ingredients
3/4 teaspoon garlic powder
1 teaspoon salt
1/2 teaspoon pepper
4 pounds pork spareribs
1 (10.75 ounce) can condensed tomato soup, undiluted
1 small onion, chopped
1 cup water
1/2 cup light corn syrup
1/2 cup ketchup
1/4 cup cider vinegar
2 tablespoons Worcestershire sauce
2 teaspoons chili powder
1 teaspoon hot pepper sauce
1/2 teaspoon ground cinnamon

Directions
1. Combine garlic powder, salt and pepper; rub onto both sides of ribs. Place in a in a baking pan. Bake on Hi for 30-35 minutes; drain off fat.
2. Combine sauce ingredients; pour over ribs. Bake 50-60 minutes longer, basting occasionally. Cut into serving-size pieces.

Beef Nacho Casserole
Makes 6 servings
Cook Time: 20 Min

Ingredients
1 pound ground beef
1 1/2 cups chunky salsa
1 (10 ounce) can whole kernel corn, drained
3/4 cup creamy salad dressing (e.g. Miracle Whip)
1 teaspoon chili powder
2 cups crushed tortilla chips
2 cups Colby cheese

Directions
1. Place ground beef in a large skillet over medium-high heat.
2. Cook, stirring to crumble, until evenly browned. Drain grease. Remove from the heat, and stir the salsa, corn, mayonnaise and chili powder into the beef. In a casserole dish, layer the ground beef mixture, tortilla chips and cheese twice, ending with cheese on top.
3. Bake on Hi for 20 minutes uncovered in the preheated oven, until cheese is melted and dish is thoroughly heated.

Black Magic Cake
Makes 24 servings
Cook Time: 35 Min

Ingredients
1 3/4 cups all-purpose flour
2 cups white sugar
3/4 cup unsweetened cocoa powder
2 teaspoons baking soda
1 teaspoon baking powder
1 teaspoon salt
2 eggs
1 cup strong brewed coffee
1 cup buttermilk
1/2 cup vegetable oil
1 teaspoon vanilla extract

Directions
1. Grease and flour two round cake pans.
2. In large bowl combine flour, sugar, cocoa, baking soda, baking powder and salt. Make a well in the center.
3. Add eggs, coffee, buttermilk, oil and vanilla. Beat for 2 minutes on medium speed. Batter will be thin. Pour into prepared pans.
4. Bake on Hi for 30 to 40 minutes, or until toothpick inserted into center of cake comes out clean.

5. Cool for 10 minutes, then remove from pans and finish cooling on a wire rack. Fill and frost as desired.

Brown Sugar and Pineapple Glazed Ham
Makes 20 servings
Cook Time: 1 Hr 30 Min

Ingredients
1 (6 pound) fully-cooked, bone-in ham
1 fresh pineapple
2 (6 ounce) cans pineapple juice
1 cup brown sugar

Directions
1. Place the ham, cut side down, into a roasting pan.
2. Cut the skin off the pineapple with a sharp knife and cut out any brown spots of skin left behind. Slice the pineapple into 1/2-inch slices and cut the cores out of the slices. Pin the slices onto the ham with toothpicks.
3. Bake ham on Hi until a meat thermometer inserted into the thickest part of the ham reads 140 degrees F (60 degrees C), 1 1/2 to 2 hours.
4. While the ham is baking, mix the pineapple juice and brown sugar in a microwave-safe ceramic or glass bowl and microwave on medium power until the glaze is boiling and slightly thickened. Work carefully because the glaze will be sticky and very hot.
5. Pour about half the glaze evenly over the ham and pineapple about 1 hour before the end of baking; pour the rest over the ham about 30 minutes before the end of baking.

Burrito Pie

Makes 16 servings
Cook Time: 30 Min

Ingredients

2 pounds ground beef
1 onion, chopped
2 teaspoons minced garlic
1 (2 ounce) can black olives, sliced
1 (4 ounce) can diced green chili peppers
1 (10 ounce) can diced tomatoes with green chile peppers
1 (16 ounce) jar taco sauce
2 (16 ounce) cans refried beans
12 (8 inch) flour tortillas
9 ounces shredded Colby cheese

Directions

1. In a large skillet over medium heat, saute the ground beef for 5 minutes.
2. Add the onion and garlic, and saute for 5 more minutes. Drain any excess fat, if desired. Mix in the olives, green chile peppers, tomatoes with green chile peppers, taco sauce and refried beans. Stir mixture thoroughly, reduce heat to low, and let simmer for 15 to 20 minutes.
3. Spread a thin layer of the meat mixture in the bottom of a 4 quart casserole dish. Cover with a layer of tortillas followed by more meat mixture, then a layer of cheese. Repeat tortilla, meat, cheese pattern until all the tortillas are used, topping off with a layer of meat mixture and cheese.
4. Bake on Hi for 20 to 30 minutes until cheese is slightly brown and bubbly.

Cheesy Chicken Quesadillas

Makes 8 servings
Cook Time: 5 Min

Ingredients

1 pound skinless, boneless chicken breast, cut into cubes
1 (10.75 ounce) can Campbell's® Condensed Cream of Chicken Soup
1/2 cup Pace® Thick & Chunky Salsa
1/2 cup shredded Monterey Jack cheese
1 teaspoon chili powder
8 flour tortillas (8-inch), warmed

Directions

1. Cook the chicken in a 10-inch nonstick skillet over medium-high heat until it's well browned and cooked through, stirring often.
2. Stir in the soup, salsa, cheese and chili powder and cook until the mixture is hot and bubbling.
3. Place the tortillas onto baking sheets. Spread about 1/3 cup chicken mixture on half of each tortilla to within 1/2-inch of the edge. Brush the edges of the tortillas with water. Fold the tortillas over the filling and press the edges to seal.
4. Bake on Hi for 5 minutes or until the filling is hot. Cut the quesadillas into wedges and serve with additional salsa.

Cordon Bleu Casserole

Makes 6 servings
Cook Time: 25 Min

Ingredients

2 cups cubed fully cooked ham
4 cups cubed cooked turkey
1 cup shredded Swiss cheese
1 large onion, chopped
1/3 cup butter or margarine
1/3 cup all-purpose flour
1/8 teaspoon ground mustard
1/8 teaspoon ground nutmeg
1 3/4 cups milk
1 1/2 cups soft bread crumbs
1/2 cup shredded Swiss cheese
1/4 cup butter or margarine, melted

Directions

1. In a nonstick skillet, saute ham for 4-5 minutes or until browned; drain and pat dry. In a greased baking dish, layer the turkey, cheese and ham; set aside.
2. In a saucepan, saute the onion in butter until tender. Stir in the flour, mustard and nutmeg until blended. Gradually stir in milk. Bring to a boil; cook and stir for 2 minutes or until thickened.
3. Pour over ham. Combine topping ingredients; sprinkle over the top. Bake, uncovered, on Hi for 25-30 minutes or until golden brown and bubbly.

Country Club Prime Rib
Makes 8 servings
Cook Time: 2 Hrs

Ingredients
5 pounds prime rib roast
1 cup kosher salt
2 teaspoons garlic powder
1 tablespoon coarsely ground black pepper

Directions
1. Trim the prime rib roast of excess fat and any connective tissue. Lightly score the entire roast in a criss-cross pattern (about 1/8 inch deep).
2. In a small bowl, mix together the kosher salt, garlic powder, and black pepper. Rub the mixture into the roast until it develops a crust. Really pack it on.
3. Place the roast into a roasting pan, and pour water into the bottom of the pan to 1/2 inch deep. Cover the roast with a lid or aluminum foil.
4. Roast on Hi for about 1 1/2 to 2 hours, then check the internal temperature using a meat thermometer. The internal temperature should be at least 145 degrees F (63 degrees C).
5. Hold the roast in an oven at 200 degrees F (110 degrees C) until ready to carve. Let stand for a few minutes before carving if not holding.

Cranberry Pumpkin Muffins
Makes 12 servings
Cook Time: 20 Min

Ingredients
2 cups all-purpose flour
3/4 cup brown sugar, packed
2 teaspoons baking powder
1/4 teaspoon baking soda
1/2 teaspoon salt
1 teaspoon ground cinnamon
1/4 teaspoon ground ginger
1/8 teaspoon ground cloves
1/8 teaspoon ground nutmeg
1 cup canned unsweetened pumpkin puree
2 eggs, lightly beaten
1/2 cup butter, melted
1/4 cup buttermilk
2 teaspoons vanilla extract
1 (8 ounce) package dried, sweetened cranberries

Directions
1. Grease or place paper muffin cups in a 12 cup muffin tin.
2. Mix the flour, brown sugar, baking powder, baking soda, salt, cinnamon, ginger, cloves, and nutmeg together in a mixing bowl.
3. Beat the canned pumpkin, eggs, butter, buttermilk, and vanilla together in another large mixing bowl. Gradually beat in the flour mixture until well blended. Stir in the dried cranberries until evenly blended. Spoon batter into muffin tins about 3/4 full.
4. Bake on Hi until a toothpick inserted in the middle of a muffin comes out clean, 20 to 25 minutes. 3 minutes before turning out from pan. Serve warm or at room temperature.

Cranberry Stuffed Turkey Breasts
Makes 10 servings
Cook Time: 1 Hr

Ingredients
1 (12 ounce) package herb-seasoned bread stuffing mix
2 skinless boneless turkey breasts
1 cup chopped pecans
2 (8 ounce) packages dried, sweetened cranberries
2 tablespoons olive oil
6 lettuce leaves
1/2 cup pecan halves

Directions
1. Prepare stuffing mix according to package directions. Set aside to cool.
2. With a sharp knife, butterfly breasts open to lay flat. Place each breast between two sheets of waxed paper, and flatten with a mallet. Spread the prepared stuffing to within 1/4 inch of the edge of each breast.
3. Sprinkle each one with chopped pecans and dried cranberries, reserving some of the cranberries for garnish. Roll up tightly in a jellyroll style, starting with the long end.
4. Tuck in ends, and tie in sections with string, about 4 sections around the middle and one running the length of the roll to secure the ends.
5. Heat olive oil in a large cast iron skillet over medium-high heat. Carefully brown rolls on all sides.
6. Place in baking dish and bake on Hi for 1 hour, or until the internal temperature is at 170 degrees F (78 degrees C) when taken with a meat thermometer.
7. Do not let these get overly dry. 5. Allow rolls to set for 15 minutes before removing string, and slicing into 1/2 to 3/4 inch circles.

Eggnog Cake

Makes 10 servings
Cook Time: 1 Hr 5 Min

Ingredients

2 cups all-purpose flour
1 tablespoon baking powder
1 teaspoon salt
1 teaspoon ground nutmeg
1/4 teaspoon ground ginger
1 cup white sugar
1/4 cup butter
1/4 cup shortening
2 eggs
1 teaspoon rum flavored extract
3/4 cup milk

Directions

1. Grease and flour a loaf pan. Sift together the flour, baking powder, salt, nutmeg, and ginger; set aside.
2. In a large bowl, cream together sugar, butter, and shortening until light and fluffy. Blend in the eggs one at a time, then stir in the rum extract. Beat in the flour mixture alternately with the milk, mixing just until incorporated. Pour batter into prepared pan.
3. Bake on Hi for 65 to 70 minutes, or until a toothpick inserted into the center of the cake comes out clean.

Glazed Corned Beef

Makes 7 servings
Cook Time: 3 Hrs

Ingredients

4 1/2 pounds corned beef, rinsed
1 cup water
1 cup apricot preserves
1/4 cup brown sugar
2 tablespoons soy sauce

Directions

1. Coat a large pan with non-stick cooking spray. Place corned beef in dish and add water.
2. Cover tightly with aluminum foil and bake on Hi for 2 hours; drain liquid.
3. In a small bowl combine apricot preserves, brown sugar, and soy sauce. Spread the apricot mixture evenly over the corned beef.
4. Bake on Hi uncovered for 25 to 30 more minutes, or until the meat is tender; basting occasionally with pan drippings.
5. Slice corned beef across grain and serve.

Guinness Corned Beef

Makes 16 servings
Cook Time: 2 Hrs 30 Min

Ingredients

4 pounds corned beef brisket
1 cup brown sugar
1 (12 fluid ounce) can or bottle Irish stout beer (e.g. Guinness®)

Directions

1. Rinse the beef completely and pat dry.
2. Place the brisket in a roasting pan. Rub the brown sugar on the corned beef to coat entire beef, including the bottom. Pour the bottle of stout beer around, and gently over the beef to wet the sugar.
3. Cover, and bake on Hi for 2 1/2 hours. Allow to rest 5 minutes before slicing.

Honey Glazed Ham

Makes 15 servings
Cook Time: 1 Hr 15 Min

Ingredients

1 (5 pound) ready-to-eat ham
1/4 cup whole cloves
1/4 cup dark corn syrup
2 cups honey
2/3 cup butter

Directions

1. Score ham, and stud with the whole cloves. Place ham in foil lined pan.
2. In the top half of a double boiler, heat the corn syrup, honey and butter. Keep glaze warm while baking ham.
3. Brush glaze over ham, and bake on Hi for 1 hour and 15 minutes. Baste ham every 10 to 15 minutes with the honey glaze.
4. During the last 4 to 5 minutes of baking put ham under oven broiler to caramelize the glaze. Remove from oven, and let sit a few minutes before serving.

Leftover Thanksgiving Turkey Pot Pie
Makes 6 servings
Cook Time: 25 Min

Ingredients
2 1/2 cups chopped cooked turkey
1 (10.75 ounce) can condensed cream of chicken soup
1 (15.5 ounce) can whole kernel corn, drained
1 (14.5 ounce) can sliced carrots, drained
1 (15 ounce) can sliced white potatoes, drained and chopped
1/4 cup chicken stock
salt and ground black pepper to taste
2 1/4 cups biscuit baking mix (such as Bisquick®)
2/3 cup milk

Directions
1. Grease a baking dish.
2. In a large bowl, gently mix together the cooked turkey, cream of chicken soup, corn, carrots, potatoes, and chicken stock until thoroughly combined.
3. Season to taste with salt and black pepper. Transfer the mixture to the prepared baking dish. In a second bowl, mix the baking mix and milk to form a dough; roll the dough out to a rectangle on a floured work surface.
4. Place the dough on top of the baking dish.
5. Bake on Hi until the filling is bubbling and the biscuit dough topping is browned, about 25 minutes.

Maple Glazed Turkey Roast
Makes 6 servings
Cook Time: 1 Hr 30 Min

Ingredients
1 (3 pound) boneless turkey breast roast, thawed
1/2 cup pure maple syrup, or more as needed
1 teaspoon liquid smoke flavoring (optional)
1 teaspoon ground paprika
1/2 teaspoon salt
1/2 teaspoon pepper
1/2 teaspoon garlic powder
1/2 teaspoon onion powder
1/2 teaspoon dried crushed thyme
1 pinch cayenne pepper, or to taste

Directions
1. Remove the plastic netting and wrap from the turkey roast, if any, but leave on string netting. (Remove and discard gravy packet, if any).
2. Rinse the turkey, and pat dry with paper towels.

3. Mix together the maple syrup, smoke flavoring, paprika, salt, pepper, garlic powder, onion powder, thyme, and cayenne pepper in a bowl, stirring to combine well. Brush the syrup mixture all over the turkey roast.
4. Place the roast, skin side up, on a baking rack set in a roasting pan. Roast on Hi basting occasionally, until the roast is golden brown and a meat thermometer inserted into the center of the roast reads 170 degrees F (75 degrees C).
5. Roasting time is about 1 1/2 hours. Wrap the roast in foil, and let stand 10 minutes before removing the string netting for slicing.

Mexican Cornbread
Makes 6 servings
Cook Time: 1 Hr

Ingredients
1 cup butter, melted
1 cup white sugar
4 eggs
1 (15 ounce) can cream-style corn
1/2 (4 ounce) can chopped green chile peppers, drained
1/2 cup shredded Monterey Jack cheese
1/2 cup shredded Cheddar cheese
1 cup all-purpose flour
1 cup yellow cornmeal
4 teaspoons baking powder
1/4 teaspoon salt

Directions
1. Lightly grease a 9x13 inch baking dish.
2. In a large bowl, beat together butter and sugar. Beat in eggs one at a time. Blend in cream corn, chiles, Monterey Jack and Cheddar cheese.
3. In a separate bowl, stir together flour, cornmeal, baking powder and salt. Add flour mixture to corn mixture; stir until smooth. Pour batter into prepared pan.
4. Bake on Hi for 1 hour, until a toothpick inserted into center of the pan comes out clean.

Pork Loin Roast with Herbed Pepper Rub
Makes 8 servings

Ingredients
1 (3 pound) boneless pork loin roast
Herbed Pepper Rub:
2 tablespoons cracked black pepper
2 tablespoons grated Parmesan cheese
2 teaspoons dried basil
2 teaspoons dried rosemary
2 teaspoons dried thyme
1/4 teaspoon garlic powder
1/4 teaspoon salt

Directions
1. Pat pork dry with paper towel. In small bowl, combine all rub ingredients well and apply to all surfaces of the pork roast.
2. Place roast in a shallow pan and roast on Hi for 1 to 1-1/4 hours (18 to 20 minutes per pound), until internal temperature on a thermometer reads 150 degrees F.
3. Remove roast from oven; let rest until temperature reaches 160 degrees F, about 10 minutes before slicing to serve.

Prime Rib and Potatoes
Makes 2 servings
Cook Time: 2 Hrs

Ingredients
1 tablespoon olive or vegetable oil
1 small garlic clove, minced
3 pounds prime rib roast (standing rib roast)
2 large baking potatoes

Directions
1. Combine the oil and garlic; rub evenly over roast. Place roast, fat side up, in a small roasting pan. Place a potato on each side of roast.
2. Bake, uncovered, on Hi for 2 to 2-1/2 hours until meat reaches desired doneness (for medium-rare, a meat thermometer should read 145 degrees F; medium, 160 degrees F; well done, 170 degrees F). Let stand for 10 minutes before carving.

Prime Rib Roast
Makes 16 servings
Cook Time: 2 Hrs

Ingredients
3 teaspoons grated fresh ginger root
1/3 cup orange marmalade
4 cloves garlic, minced
3 tablespoons soy sauce
2 tablespoons brown sugar
1/4 teaspoon hot pepper sauce
1 tablespoon mustard powder
1 cup beer
1 (8 pound) prime rib roast
1/4 cup olive oil
ground black pepper to taste

Directions
1. Mix together the ginger, marmalade, garlic, soy sauce, brown sugar, hot sauce, and mustard. Stir in the beer. Prick holes all over the roast with a 2 pronged fork. Pour marinade over roast. Cover, and refrigerate for at least 2 hours, basting at least twice.
2. Place roast in a roasting pan.
3. Pour about 1 cup of marinade into the roasting pan, and discard remaining marinade. Pour olive oil over roast, and season with freshly ground black pepper.
4. Insert a roasting thermometer into the middle of the roast, making sure that the thermometer does not touch any bone. Cover roasting pan with aluminum foil, and seal edges tightly around pan.
5. Cook roast on Hi for 1 hour. After the first hour, remove the aluminum foil. Baste, reduce heat by 1 or 2 levels and continue roasting for 1 more hour.
6. The thermometer reading should be at least 140 degrees F (60 degrees C) for medium-rare, and 170 degrees F (76 degrees C) for well done.
7. Remove roasting pan from oven, place aluminum foil over roast, and let rest for about 30 minutes before slicing.

Pumpkin Muffins
Makes 36 servings
Cook Time: 35 Min

Ingredients
1 1/2 cups raisins
4 3/4 cups all-purpose flour
4 cups white sugar
1 1/2 teaspoons baking powder
1 1/2 teaspoons baking soda
1 1/2 teaspoons salt
1 1/2 teaspoons nutmeg
1 1/2 teaspoons cinnamon
1 1/2 teaspoons ground cloves
6 eggs
1 (29 ounce) can pumpkin
1 cup unsweetened applesauce
1 cup chopped walnuts

Directions
1. Grease three 12 cup muffin pans, or line with paper muffin liners. Soak raisins in hot water for ten minutes to plump, then drain.
2. In a large bowl, combine the flour, sugar, baking powder, baking soda, salt, nutmeg, cinnamon, and ground cloves. In a separate bowl, mix the eggs, pumpkin, and applesauce, until smooth.
3. Add this mixture to the dry ingredients and stir thoroughly to make a smooth batter. Stir the raisins and walnuts into the batter. Spoon batter into the prepared muffin cups.
4. Bake on Hi for 30 to 35 minutes in the preheated oven, or until a toothpick inserted into the center comes out clean.

Pumpkin Pie
Makes 8 servings
Cook Time: 1 Hr

Ingredients
1 (9 inch) unbaked deep dish pie crust
3/4 cup white sugar
1 teaspoon ground cinnamon
1/2 teaspoon salt
1/2 teaspoon ground ginger
1/4 teaspoon ground cloves
2 eggs
1 (15 ounce) can Pure Pumpkin
1 (12 fluid ounce) can Evaporated Milk

Directions
1. Combine sugar, salt, cinnamon, ginger and cloves in small bowl.

2. Beat eggs lightly in large bowl. Stir in pumpkin and sugar-spice mixture. Gradually stir in evaporated milk. Pour into pie shell.
3. Bake on Hi for 15 minutes. Reduce temperature 1 level and bake for 40 to 50 minutes or until knife inserted near center comes out clean.
4. Cool on wire rack for 2 hours. Serve immediately or refrigerate. (Do not freeze as this will cause the crust to separate from the filling.)

Roast Turkey with Herb Stuffing
Makes 12 servings

Ingredients
3 tablespoons butter
1 large onion (chopped)
1 bag Savory Herb Stuffing
3/4 cup Low Sodium Chicken Broth
1 large egg (lightly beaten)
1 (12 pound) fresh turkey
1 tablespoon Canola Oil
Iodized Sea Salt

Directions
1. In a medium-size saucepan, melt the butter over moderate heat. Add the onion and cook for 5 minutes or until tender.
2. Add Low Sodium Chicken Broth bringing mixture to a boil. Remove from the heat. In a very large bowl, combine Savory Herb Stuffing Mix and stir in the onion mixture.
3. Rinse turkey, drain and pat dry. Remove neck and giblets; set aside to make the gravy. Stuff and truss turkey, place breast-side-up on a rack in a large roasting pan.
4. Brush with Canola Oil top with Sea Salt. Insert roasting thermometer in turkey thigh without touching bone. Roast turkey on Hi for 3 to 3 1/2 hours or until thermometer registers 180 degrees F, basting often and covering with foil to prevent overbrowning if necessary.
5. Let turkey stand for 15 to 20 minutes before carving. 3. Meanwhile, cook neck and giblets for gravy.
6. Reserve 2 tablespoons of the pan drippings from roast turkey for giblet gravy. Prepare gravy. Carve turkey and serve with stuffing and gravy.

Stuffed Red Bell Peppers
Makes 4 servings
Cook Time: 1 Hr

Ingredients
1 cup uncooked brown rice
2 1/4 cups water
4 red bell peppers, tops and seeds removed
1 teaspoon olive oil
1/4 onion, chopped
2 cloves garlic, chopped
1 (15 ounce) can black-eyed peas, rinsed and drained
2 large Swiss chard leaves, chopped
salt and black pepper to taste

Directions
1. Bring the brown rice and water to a boil in a saucepan over high heat. Reduce the heat to medium-low, cover, and simmer until the rice is tender and the liquid has been absorbed, 45 to 50 minutes.
2. Spray a baking sheet with cooking spray.
3. Place the red peppers on the prepared baking sheet, and bake on Hi until tender, about 15 minutes.
4. Heat the olive oil in a skillet over medium heat, and cook and stir the onion and garlic until the onion is translucent, about 5 minutes. Stir in the black-eyed peas and chard. Bring the mixture to a simmer, and cook until the chard is wilted, 5 to 8 minutes.
5. Mix in the cooked brown rice, sprinkle with salt and pepper to taste, and lightly stuff the mixture into the red peppers. Serve hot.

Stuffed Turkey
Makes 12 servings
Cook Time: 3 Hrs 45 Min

Ingredients
2 large onions, chopped
2 celery ribs, chopped
1/2 pound fresh mushrooms, sliced
1/2 cup butter
1 (14.5 ounce) can chicken broth
1/3 cup minced fresh parsley
2 teaspoons rubbed sage
1 teaspoon salt
1 teaspoon poultry seasoning
1/2 teaspoon pepper
12 cups unseasoned stuffing cubes
Warm water
1 (14 pound) turkey
Melted butter

Directions
1. In a large skillet, saute the onions, celery and mushrooms in butter until tender. Add broth and seasonings; mix well. Place bread cubes in a large bowl; add mushroom mixture and toss to coat. Stir in enough warm water to reach desired moistness.
2. Just before baking, loosely stuff turkey. Place any remaining stuffing in a greased baking dish; cover and refrigerate until ready to bake. Skewer turkey openings; tie drumsticks together with kitchen string.
3. Place breast side up on a rack in a roasting pan. Brush with melted butter. 3. Bake turkey, uncovered, on Hi for 3-3/4 to 4-1/2 hours or until a meat thermometer reads 180 for the turkey and 165 for the stuffing, basting occasionally with pan drippings. (Cover loosely with foil if turkey browns too quickly.)
4. Bake additional stuffing, covered, for 30-40 minutes. Uncover; bake 10 minutes longer or until lightly browned. Cover turkey with foil and let stand for 20 minutes before removing stuffing and carving. If desired, thicken pan drippings for gravy.

Sweet Potato Pudding
Makes 4 servings
Cook Time: 30 Min

Ingredients
1 (29 ounce) can sweet potatoes
2 eggs, lightly beaten
1 cup packed brown sugar
1 cup milk
1/4 cup melted butter
2 teaspoons lemon juice
1/4 teaspoon ground ginger
1/4 teaspoon ground cloves
1/2 teaspoon ground cinnamon
1/2 teaspoon salt

Directions
1. Grease a baking dish.
2. Combine sweet potatoes and eggs in a medium bowl. Beat in the brown sugar, milk, butter, lemon juice, ginger, cloves, cinnamon, salt. Pour into prepared dish.
3. Bake on Hi until hot and golden brown on top, about 30 minutes.

CPSIA information can be obtained at www.ICGtesting.com
Printed in the USA
LVOW091406260213

321773LV00001B/2/P